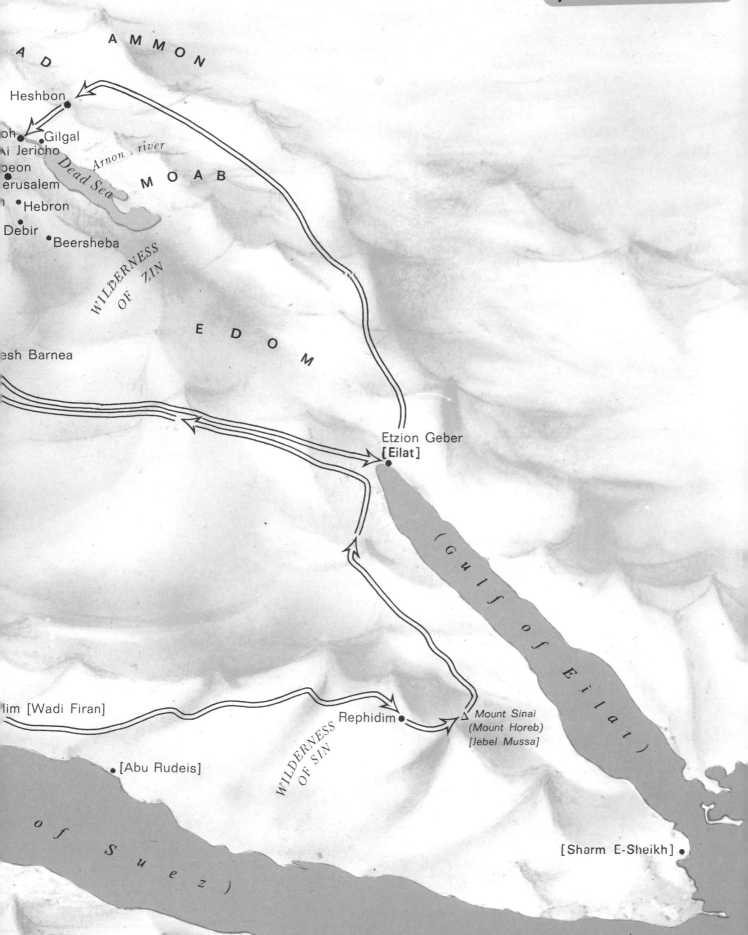

MOSES

MOSES

WHERE IT ALL BEGAN

by MOSHE PEARLMAN

PHOTOGRAPHY BY DAVID HARRIS

GENERAL EDITOR MORDECAI RAANAN

ABELARD-SCHUMAN   NEW YORK

An Intext Publisher

First American Edition 1974
Abelard-Schuman Limited, 257 Park Avenue South, New York, New York 10010.

Copyright © 1973 by Nateev Ltd. P.O.Box 6048, Tel-Aviv, Israel.

An adaptation of the title THE FIRST DAYS OF ISRAEL by Moshe Pearlman

Library of Congress Catalog Card Number: 73-21320

ISBN: 0-200-00138-8

Published on the same day in Canada by Longman Canada Limited.

ACKNOWLEDGMENTS and thanks are due to the following institutions and persons for having kindly permitted their exhibits to be photographed: Department of Antiquities and Museums, Ministry of Education and Culture, Jerusalem; Rockefeller Museum, pages 21, 130–31, 177; Israel Museum, pages 122, 184, 198; The Jewish National and University Library, Jerusalem, pages 152–53; The Library of St. Thoros, The Armenian Orthodox Patriarchate, Jerusalem, pages 64, 72, 116; U.S. Information Service, The Embassy of the U.S.A., Tel Aviv, page 69; The Pierpont Morgan Library, New York, N.Y., pages 181, 201; E. M. Cross, Jr., Harvard University, pages 126–27. Photographs by Uzi Paz, page 104; by Werner Braun, page 106; by other photographers, pages 13, 14–15, 25, 26–27, 125, 128.

Design Consultant, Gad Ulman

Printed in Israel

CONTENTS

CHAPTER 1 THE CHILD UNDER SENTENCE OF DEATH

In which a cruel Pharaoh orders that all Hebrew baby boys be drowned, but the infant Moses is rescued by the king's own daughter.

Moses was one of the greatest leaders who ever lived. He was a giant of his times, and of all times. Yet no one could have started life under a more terrifying handicap: he was sentenced to death at birth! Nor could any life have been marked by such strange paradox. Born to a family of slaves, he was brought up in the palace of a king. Educated as a prince, he became a revolutionary. Living under the roof of a tough dictator whose officials were equally heartless and cruel, the young Moses managed to preserve a natural sense of fair play. Indeed, so strong was his feeling for justice that he acted on impulse to correct a wrong, and was again sentenced to death. He escaped, and fell sharply from the luxurious heights of a city nobleman to the primitive life of a desert shepherd.

Torn as a baby from his people and their religion, he it was who set them free, established their faith and molded them into a nation. Afflicted with a stammer, he spoke words of exalted wisdom. A man of lofty thought, he was also practical and down to earth. A statesman of vision, he was, too, a fighter, who planned with care and battled with courage. At a time when popular resistance was unheard of, he led a revolt, the first revolt of slaves in recorded history. His enormous gifts were crowned above all by a nobility of ideas and ideals, so that to this day, some three thousand three hundred years later, we in the western world, whether Jewish or Christian, seek to live by the standards he set.

His life was packed with adventure, and his adventures started when he was a baby of three months. This happened in Egypt at the beginning of the 13th century BC. Egypt at that time was not as powerful as she had been, but she was still a country of wealth and influence. Only one other political and military power in the region, the Hittite empire in the north, could compete with her for control of the Middle East. (Between these two rival empires lay the land of Canaan, peopled by a variety of mixed groups, each with its petty king. All were almost always under the control either of Egypt in the south or of the neighboring empire in the north. This land, Canaan, was the Promised Land of the Israelites.)

*the daughter of Pharaoh...
saw the basket... and lo,
the babe was crying... she
named him Moses*

(*Exodus 2:5, 6, 10*)

Ancient wall paintings showing the child Moses
being taken from his basket in the water by
the Egyptian princess, and brought to the river bank.
These scenes decorated the 3rd century AD synagogue
of Dura-Europos, a noted town in Babylonia.
They were discovered during
an archaeological dig in 1932.

RICHES AND SLAVERY

Egypt was ruled by a king. (The local title
for "King" was "Pharaoh.") He was a sole
dictator, with the power of life and death over
his subjects. At his command were a con-
siderable army, equipped with chariots; stern
administrators who kept a tight rein on the
people; artists who fashioned treasures of
beauty for the royal family; and clever
architects and engineers who built splendid
palaces and temples to glorify the Pharaoh.

The capital was indeed marked by riches
and luxury, intended as a living monument to
the might of the ruler. It was a showplace to
impress his own countrymen, as well as
foreign diplomats and distinguished visitors,
with the greatness of Egypt. But beyond this
site of splendor, the rest of the country was
filled with vast human misery. The Egyptian
people themselves were poor, but far worse off
were the slaves. These were mostly men,
women and children who had been captured
in battle by the Egyptians. They had to work
hard — the women and children as servants,
the men on tough construction jobs — without
pay and without freedom, until they died.

11

Then Pharaoh commanded..., 'Every son that is born to the Hebrews you shall cast into the Nile' (Exodus 1:22)

The river Nile, the great African waterway which runs through Egypt. It is so wide in parts that it was often called "The sea of the Nile". At the time of Moses' birth, there was an order by the Pharaoh that all new-born Hebrew boys should be thrown into this river and drowned.

At a level just above the captive slaves were certain oppressed communities who also belonged to the State — the property of the Pharaoh. They were called State slaves, or bondsmen. They usually lived as a group in a particular district, and scratched out a meager living from crops and cattle. But at any moment the Pharaoh could order all or some of the men to be rounded up and pressed into forced-labor gangs. They were then put to work quarrying stones, making bricks and building some temple or monument which he had decided to erect. One such State slave community were the Hebrews, members of the twelve tribes descended from the Patriarchs Abraham, Isaac and Jacob. ("Patriarch" means father or chief of a family, tribe or race.)

Abraham was the first to enter into a Covenant, or solemn agreement, with the one invisible God. To him the Lord made the promise of a land for his descendants. The Covenant and the promise were re-affirmed with Abraham's son Isaac, and with Isaac's son Jacob. Jacob had twelve sons, and they fathered the Hebrew tribes. (Jacob was also given the name "Israel", and the Hebrews were thus known collectively, as the Children of Israel or Israelites, as well, of course, as members of the House of Jacob.) It was the descendants of Jacob's sons who were now suffering slave conditions in 13th century Egypt.

THE CRUEL TYRANT

Their fortunes had indeed tumbled. Three hundred years earlier, a young Hebrew, Joseph, beloved son of Jacob, had saved Egypt from starvation. How he reached Egypt from his home in Canaan and rose to become chief adviser to the Pharaoh is one of the most romantic stories in the Bible. Foreseeing a drought in the region, he advised the king to store grain during the fruitful years. When famine struck, Egypt was the only country in the area with reserve supplies of food, and Joseph was appointed governor of the land. He eventually brought his father and brothers, together with their families, to Egypt. With the Pharaoh's blessing, he settled them in the "land of Goshen", situated in northeastern Egypt close to what is today the Suez Canal.

12

The pyramids were huge stone burial monuments for the ancient Pharaohs, and were built by slaves. This is one of the three pyramids of Gizeh. It stands 450 feet high on an almost square base of 750 by 750 feet. The 5th century BC Greek historian Herodotus estimated that it took 100,000 slaves 20 years to build it.

So they made the people of Israel serve with rigour...

It was from quarries like this
that the huge stones were
extracted by slave labor and used
for the construction of the pyramids.

There they lived as a tribal community, pasturing their flocks and pursuing a quiet, untroubled and prosperous existence. In one way alone did they differ from their neighbors. The Egyptians were pagans, worshipping idols. The Hebrews remembered and remained faithful to the Covenant of their Patriarchs with God. This set them apart.

We know little of what happened to them in the period following the death of Joseph. We know only the bare fact that "the descendants of Israel were fruitful and increased greatly; they multiplied and grew exceedingly strong; so that the land was filled with them" (Exodus 1:7). It is clear, however, that at some stage during those three centuries they suffered a tragic change in treatment by the Egyptian rulers. They lost their freedom and were forced into slavery.

Some modern scholars believe that this happened when the Hyksos regime came to an end. The Hyksos were a northern people who had thundered down through Canaan and invaded Egypt. They were armed with powerful new weapons — the horse-drawn chariot and a long-range bow — and they

16

Making mud bricks. This was one of the tasks forced upon the Israelite slaves, who had to complete a heavy quota each day.

soon overran the Egyptian defenses. For more than a hundred years they were the masters of Egypt, building a new capital, called Avaris, at the northern edge of Goshen. This was where the Hebrews soon came to settle, and it is suggested that Joseph's royal friend was a Hyksos ruler.

When Avaris was captured and the Hyksos driven out, the new Pharaoh must have dealt harshly with the Israelites and other foreign tribes who had been friendly with the Hyksos. In time, however, as Pharaoh followed Pharaoh, and as most of the foreign communities became "Egyptianized", adopting the pagan customs of the rest of the population, hatred of them disappeared. But hatred of the Israelites remained; for they continued to be a distinctive community, clinging to their belief in the one invisible God. This the Egyptians could not understand. Lack of understanding led to suspicion, and suspicion to dislike. It was therefore a popular move on the part of the Pharaohs to persecute the Hebrews. It was also profitable: the Hebrews became a royal reservoir of forced labor for the construction of monuments and cities. Despite

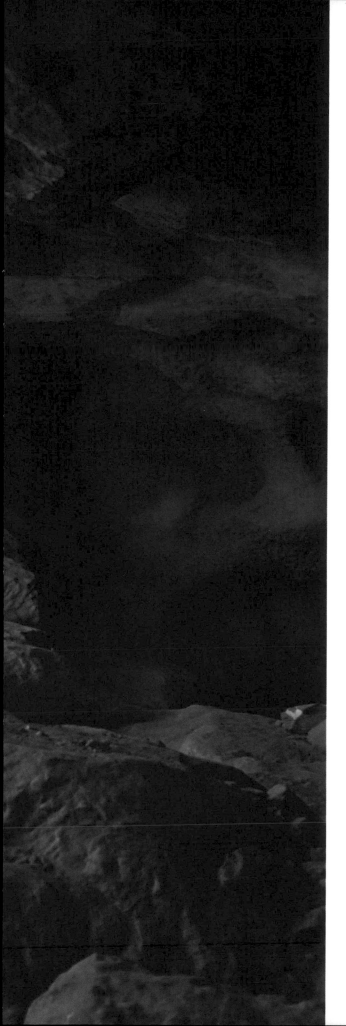

This was a quarry where Semitic slaves were put to work by the ancient Egyptian rulers mining turquoise, a greenish-blue precious stone. It is situated at a place called Serabit el-Khadem, at the western edge of the Sinai desert.

this, the Hebrews somehow managed to multiply and grow "exceedingly strong", and this made the Egyptians hate them even more. By the time Moses was born, they were a community of State slaves in bond to a new Pharaoh "who did not know Joseph", and who "said to his people, 'Behold, the people of Israel are too many and too mighty for us' ..." And so he "set taskmasters over them to afflict them with heavy burdens; and they built for Pharaoh store cities, Pithom and Raamses" (Exodus I:11).

THE MAIDEN AND THE BABY

The Pharaoh at this time is believed to have been Sethos I (1309–1290 BC), father of the far better known Rameses II. The city of Pithom built by the Hebrew slaves was at the southern edge of Goshen, a few miles south-west of today's Ismailia on the Suez Canal. The city of Raamses lay at the northern edge of Goshen, southwest of today's Port Said. The site of Raamses was none other than that of the ancient Hyksos capital Avaris, and it was now beginning to be rebuilt by the Hebrews at the order of Sethos I. His son

19

Rameses II completed the reconstruction of this city and renamed it after himself, and this is the name, though in the slightly altered form of Raamses, that appears in the biblical Book of Exodus. (Its name was changed to Tanis two centuries later, and in Numbers [13:22] and in Psalms [78:12, 43] it is also referred to as Zoan.)

One would have thought that the Pharaoh was giving enough vent to his hatred of the Hebrews by putting them to harsh slave labor. One would also have thought that he would wish to serve his economic interests by at least keeping them alive, even at the lowest level of existence, as previous Pharaohs had done. But hatred of a race, a nation, a religious minority or any collective group is always irrational and often leads to contradictions. We have seen this from the behavior of certain dictators throughout history, right down to Hitler and his Nazis in our own day. Thus, for Pharaoh Sethos, cruelty to the Hebrews was not sufficient. They had to be wiped out, even though this meant losing a large labor force.

However, he did not wish to delay progress on his building projects, and so he ordered the death not of the working adults but of their male infants. All Hebrew baby boys were to be killed at birth. This would guarantee the eventual disappearance of the Hebrew community. The surviving women would become servants to the Egyptians.

The command went out from the Pharaoh's court to all the Hebrew midwives, the nurses who helped the mothers when a baby was being born: "If it is a son, you shall kill him" (Exodus I:14). The midwives took no notice of this cruel order. When they were charged with disobedience, they explained that "the Hebrew women are not like the Egyptian women; for they are vigorous" and deliver their babies "before the midwife comes to them". The Pharaoh thereupon gave the task to his own inspectors and ordered them to throw new-born Hebrew males into the river Nile.

Thus it was that the infant Moses was actually under sentence of death the moment he drew his first breath, for he was born shortly after Sethos issued his pitiless command. His father was Amram and his mother

This 16th century BC dagger, found at archaeological excavations at Lachish, in the southern Judea of today, bears one of the earliest forms of writing. It is called proto-Sinaitic. "Protos" is Greek for "first" or "original", and proto-Sinaitic is the first writing in the region to use letters instead of pictures of objects (hieroglyphs) to convey a word, a syllable or a sound.

Jochebed, of the tribe of Levi, the tribe that was most loyal to the Patriarchs' Covenant and most careful to avoid the pagan ways of the Egyptians. Jochebed promptly hid the child, and kept him hidden for three months. They were months of great anxiety for her, wondering all the while what to do to save her baby: for if he were spotted in public he would be taken and killed. She eventually decided on a plan, and when she could hide him no longer, she put it into effect.

She made a basket of bulrushes, taken from the banks of the river, and covered it with pitch to make it water-tight. Into this basket she put her baby and placed it among the reeds at the edge of the Nile. She then told her daughter Miriam to keep watch over it, from a distance, and see what would happen. It was her hope that the child would be picked up and taken into an Egyptian home, this being the only way in which his life would be spared. Miriam would take note of who the foster mother would be, try and make contact with her, follow the child's progress and perhaps after a time get him back.

The foster mother turned out to be the

This temple to the Egyptian goddess Hathor (left) was discovered at Serabit el-Khadem. It was apparently used by the Egyptian overseers of the Semitic slaves who worked in the quarries. The stone carvings (below) found in the temple are hieroglyphic inscriptions.

Pharaoh's daughter, who noticed the basket when she came down to the river with her maidens to bathe. She realized that this must be "one of the Hebrews' children" and therefore condemned by her father. But she was evidently a kind-hearted young lady, and she also seems to have been much charmed by the infant. We can imagine her taking the child from its basket, gently rocking it in her arms, fondling and cooing over it. Miriam, watching from the bank, had seen all this, and she now approached and told the princess that, if she so desired, she could find her a wet nurse to breast feed the baby. The princess seems to have been so taken with the child that she decided to adopt him, and she promptly accepted Miriam's offer. Miriam rushed home and fetched her mother. Jochebed thus nursed her own child for the Pharaoh's daughter, who brought him up as one of the princes in her father's court.

CHAPTER 2 THE PRINCE AT PHARAOH'S COURT

*In which Moses is brought up as a prince in the royal household,
and there he learns many things — and makes a shocking discovery.*

For the princes, princesses and most other members of the royal household, life at the court of Pharaoh was a life of luxury and banqueting, of pomp and stately ceremonial. They lived on a tight little island, cut off from the public. They were aware of the existence of what they considered the common people, but they were unaware of them as human beings. They might know that part of the riches they enjoyed was the product of slavery, but the lives of the slaves would not have touched them at all. They regarded themselves as a group apart, a unique and superior group, different in character and destiny from the rest of the population. They were, after all, related to the Pharaoh who — so they all believed — had been chosen by the gods to rule Egypt.

This was the insulated world in which the boy Moses grew up. However, in one broad sphere it was not insulated, and for a bright young teenager there were immense possibilities for education and enlightenment.

BEHIND THE SCENES

The Bible says little about the early life of Moses, devoting only a few sentences to his young years. But from the biblical report that he was raised by the Pharaoh's daughter, together with our behind-the-scenes understanding of how governments function, it is reasonable to surmise that Moses picked up a good deal of knowledge as a young man at the royal Egyptian court. This, after all, was the seat of national power. It was here that the king conducted affairs of State, determined policy, took major decisions affecting all the provinces in his realm. It was here that he met with his political counselors, consulted with his generals, heard reports from his administrators, received foreign ambassadors. It is of course unlikely that a young prince would have been present at such meetings and consultations, though he would have attended an occasional "audience" or "investiture" conducted by the ruler. But he would have got to know the leading men in the State, and he could, if he wished, be friendly and in frequent touch with the king's trusted advisers, chamberlains and other court officials. These men would be pleased, and flattered, to satisfy the curiosity of an

there arose a new king over Egypt...he said...'Behold, the people of Israel are too many' *(Exodus 1:8, 9)*

Statue of Rameses II, the Pharaoh at the time of the Exodus. It stands in one of the three temples at Abu Simbel, on the west bank of the Nile in the province of Aswan. Rameses built these temples as a monument to himself.

eager young prince, and to answer intelligent questions on how they handled their affairs.

But even more forthcoming, and richer sources of information to the prince, would be the aides, or assistants, to the important men who came to the palace to report to the king. We can imagine an army commander arriving to give the Pharaoh a first-hand account of a military campaign, or to inform him of threatening moves by a potential enemy — just as a present-day general may call at the White House or the Kremlin or Number Ten Downing Street to see the head of government. While he goes in to confer with the Pharaoh, his aide may sit and wait for him in the anteroom. A young prince, with the freedom of the palace, drifts in. He sees the aide, who rises, bows to royalty, and awaits the prince's pleasure. The prince is friendly, informal, and curious. What was the campaign like? How did it feel to be in battle? Which weapons proved most effective? What ingenious tactics were employed? How did they organize supplies for the forces?

These are the kinds of questions that Prince Moses might well have asked, for in the light

These four huge statues of Rameses II, 65 feet in height, flank the entrance to the main temple at Abu Simbel, which was discovered in 1812. Temple and figures were carved out of the sandstone cliffs near the river bank. The halls within are decorated with scenes illustrating the chief events in the life of this Pharaoh.

26

of his later achievements, it is reasonable to suppose that he was a remarkably gifted young man. The aide, for his part, would have been so thrilled by the friendly interest of the prince — who might be the next Pharaoh — that he would readily have given as much information to him as the general would give to the Pharaoh.

In the same casual way, the prince would chat in the palace antechambers with aides of top national administrators, political counselors, diplomats, public works officials, engineers, and receive from them not only a broad picture of what they did but also technical details.

A FABULOUS DISCOVERY

Some sixty years ago, an ancient hieroglyphic inscription (picture writing) was discovered at Wadi Hammamat in Egypt and deciphered. It told of a report to the Pharaoh by a high official that an unusually large stone had been found deep in the desert which would make a magnificent tomb, and ten thousand slaves were mobilized to dig it out and haul it to the capital. The inscription was written to glorify the ruler, so he, rather than the official who discovered the stone, gets the credit. Part of it reads: "My Majesty sent forth Amenemhat, the hereditary prince and vizier, chief of the works... in order to bring him back a block of precious stone worthy of reverence, the finest that is in the mountain... to make therefrom a sarcophagus..."

Let us conjure up the scene in the palace when news of the stone first reaches the king. Prince Amenemhat, who today would be known as Minister of Public Works, calls at the palace, and while he is recounting the discovery to the Pharaoh, his aide is in the anteroom. Along comes the young Moses, and the two get talking.

"What", asks Moses, "is all the fuss about? What great news has Amenemhat come to tell the Pharaoh?"

The aide excitedly tells him of the fabulous discovery of a huge block of stone which would make a marvelous royal tomb, and that is what his chief is telling the king.

"And how is the stone to be brought from the desert?" asks Moses.

"The slaves will bring it," says the aide.

Moses as a young man, on one of
the colored wall paintings
discovered in the ancient
synagogue of Dura-Europos.

"How many?"

"Ten thousand".

"Ten thousand!" says Moses, greatly impressed, and follows with a string of questions. How do they move the slaves on the long journey? What do they do about food and water? How do they organize staging camps en route? What tools do they use to get at the stone? How do they haul it? Do they ever have trouble with the slaves, and if so how do they deal with it?

It is feasible to speculate that such conversations might have taken place between Moses and the aides of officials when he was growing up in the palace as the adopted son of the Pharaoh's daughter. Thus, from the king and his advisers, he would have learnt about power and the way it was used. He would have seen something of the conduct of affairs at the highest level, observed the patterns of diplomacy and the process of reaching decisions and issuing orders. From the aides of top army commanders and public works officials in charge of slave projects, he would have picked up technical information on the organization and movement of large formations. Though he could hardly have known it at the time, he would in later years be applying this knowledge to a strange purpose, unique in history.

Here, perhaps, lies a clue to the solution of the mystery of how later, when Moses became a leader, he not only made the decisions but could also carry them out himself. It is something of a mystery because, in general, a leader lays down policy and his technical experts look after the practical side and get the jobs done. Indeed, certainly in the modern world, a Head of State often has not the slightest idea of how his policy is put into effect. An extreme example is the decision of President Kennedy — who was certainly no aero-space expert — to launch the program which eventually put man on the moon. But — to take a more common example — even a Prime Minister who may not know how to fire a rifle can give the order for his country to go to war. He has expert officers and men in the army, navy and air force to do the job. In the same way, it is rare for the Minister of Health in any country to be a doctor. His task is to decide the guidelines to advance his *he saw an Egyptian beating a Hebrew ... and ... he killed the Egyptian and hid him in the sand* (Exodus 2:11, 12)

Moses killed an Egyptian overseer who was beating a Hebrew slave, and he buried the body in the sand. He was to be constantly reminded of this episode, for sand dunes were part of the scenery of Sinai in which he would spend most of the rest of his life.

country's health standards, and his professional officials both provide him with advice and translate his ideas into practical deeds.

But Moses enjoyed no such help. He was alone. He had no civil service, no army officers, no police force, no professional counselors, no one with any knowledge or experience in administration or organization to assist him. He had to do it all himself, because the people he was leading, and liberating, were slaves. Thus, unlike the leader of an established government, Moses himself, until he could train assistants, had to know how to implement the policy he devised.

This, then, must be where he gained his wide range of knowledge, the technical knowledge of decision-making, of diplomacy, of organizing and moving large groups, of feeding them, securing water, working out the routes of march. His overall mission was divinely inspired; but he had to be familiar with certain basic practical techniques. These he must have acquired at the royal palace.

A DOUBLE LIFE

It seems clear from what happened later that during his young years at Pharaoh's court, Moses must have kept in touch secretly with his real family. The most probable go-between would have been his sister Miriam. Her meeting with the princess, Moses' foster mother, on the banks of the Nile, unforgettable for both, would have produced a special bond between them. It is likely that they had met discreetly from time to time and Miriam would have been favored with stories about Moses' progress. At some stage, she may have told the princess that the infant was really her brother. Making this confession would have been risky, for it would have confirmed the princess' surmise that Moses was indeed a Hebrew child, and if it got to the ears of the king, Moses and Miriam would surely be put to death. But Miriam must have guessed that the princess was devoted to the boy, would show understanding, and would keep the secret.

Several years later, when the youth was considered ripe for it, Miriam may have been instructed by Jochebed to tell Moses who he was and how he came to be in the royal palace. She would probably have told the

Now the priest of Midian had seven daughters; and they came and drew water, and filled the troughs to water their father's flock (Exodus 2:16)

Today, as in olden times, this is how women of the desert (left) carry water to their encampment. For the camels (below), there are special troughs close to springs and wells. There were troughs for animals in ancient days too, though more primitive ones.

princess what she proposed to do, secured the princess' agreement, and no doubt confronted Moses in her presence; for otherwise, the "prince", who would surely have been shocked by such a revelation, would have gone scurrying off to his "mother" for confirmation. Unless the Egyptian princess had been forewarned, and had agreed that Moses should be told the truth, Miriam would undoubtedly have found herself in very grave danger. In every way, the daughter of the Pharaoh seems to have been a most remarkable lady, kind, gentle, compassionate, quite unlike the other members of the royal household.

The news that he was really a Hebrew child, and that it was only by the purest chance that he was being brought up as a prince, must have been agonizing for the teenage Moses. Throughout his years in the palace, he would have heard the courtiers talk of the Hebrew slaves with bitter insult and cruel hatred. He now discovered that he belonged to this slave community. They were his people, and only by strange fortune had he escaped their fate. He might have reacted with horror and

Moses was keeping the flock of his father-in-law, ... and he led his flock to the west side of the wilderness, and came to Horeb, the mountain of God (Exodus 3:1)

A Bedouin shepherd with his goats and sheep in Sinai (left). When Moses roamed with Jethro's flocks in search of scrub and water, he gained an intimate knowledge of the desert through which, years later, he would lead his people to freedom. The tents (below) are made of goat's hair, the material from which desert tribes throughout the centuries have fashioned their mobile dwellings.

revulsion, deciding to drive the fearful news from his mind, forget that he had ever met Miriam. It is evident, however, that he reacted quite differently. After giving the matter serious, sober and honest thought, the unusually mature Moses clearly decided to live with this amazing new fact of his life, and to learn more about it. He must surely have had further meetings with Miriam, perhaps arranged through the princess, to hear what was happening to his community. Such reports may have stirred in him the passionate desire to lighten their burdens, and in the meantime to make full use of the broad educational opportunities afforded him at the royal court.

This period of his youth, in which he virtually lived a double life, must have been sheer torture. Outwardly, he had to behave like a carefree prince. But in his heart he carried the secret of his origins and the anguish of his people.

And the angel of the Lord appeared to him in a flame of fire out of the midst of a bush; and he looked, and lo, the bush was burning, yet it was not consumed (Exodus 3:2)

Moses listens to the divine voice from the burning bush and hears of his role of destiny. A painting on wood (left) from the Byzantine period in the Monastery of St. Catherine in southern Sinai. The event is also illustrated in the Golden Haggadah of Passover (right), produced in Spain in the early 14th century (now in the British Museum).

CHAPTER 3 THE YOUNG MAN OF THE DESERT

In which Moses is forced to escape, meets some maidens at a desert well, and hears strange words from a burning bush which affect the destiny of his people.

The Bible is silent on this. The story of his adoption as a baby moves immediately to his dramatic meeting, as a young man, with slavery. "One day, when Moses had grown up, he went out to his people and looked on their burdens; and he saw an Egyptian beating a Hebrew" (Exodus 2:11). It is unlikely that he would have gone out "to his people", concerned himself with "their burdens", worried whether or not any of them was being flogged, if he had not been aware of their suffering and of his own identity. The very fact that he went to see for himself how they were living and how they were being treated shows that he had set out with at least an idea that he might somehow be able to help them. But he could not have imagined how moved he would be by their dreadful plight, nor how angered he would be by the vicious behavior of the Egyptian slave drivers. He certainly could not have foreseen that his sight-seeing trip would end in a sudden act of violence which would force him to flee the country.

He killed the overseer who struck at the Hebrew serf, and buried his body in the sand.

Next day, however, trying to stop another fight — this time between two Hebrews — he became alarmed when one of them said: "Do you mean to kill me as you killed the Egyptian?" If news of his action had already spread, it would soon reach the ears of the Pharaoh, and, prince or no prince, he would be put to death. To attack, let alone to kill, an Egyptian overseer in order to protect a slave was punishable by execution. That was the only way the Egyptians knew to force the slaves to be disciplined and obedient, and to prevent others from interfering and endangering their slave system. Indeed, as the Bible relates, "When Pharaoh heard" what had taken place, "he sought to kill Moses." Escape was the only course, and Moses promptly fled eastwards into the Sinai desert.

After a long, hot and dusty tramp through the wilderness, he came to a well, where the shepherds in the area would come to water their flocks. Exhausted, hungry and thirsty, he drank, refreshed himself and sat down to rest. Soon, several young maidens appeared, shepherding their father's flocks. They drew water from the well, filled the nearby troughs and brought their animals to drink. While they were doing this, other Bedouin shepherds arrived. Impatient to water their flocks and thinking to take advantage of weak maidens, they pushed them away from the well, jostled their animals from the troughs and gave drink to their own flocks. The watching Moses, angered by this injustice, sprang to his feet, rushed to the well and ordered the bullying shepherds to await their turn.

The shepherds seem to have been too surprised by Moses' intervention to do anything but comply. They must have been astonished by his gallantry, for courtesy to women was not then, nor is it today, a common feature of Bedouin life. Most probably, however, they were impelled to automatic obedience by the natural note of command in Moses' voice and by his masterful bearing and appearance. He was no doubt still wearing the dress of an Egyptian nobleman, somewhat crushed and faded after his desert journey, but still impressive, and he was clearly a man of authority. The shepherds stood aside as Moses called the maidens back to the well, and he helped them draw water and fill the troughs, so that their task was quickly completed.

The girls turned out to be the daughters of Jethro (who is also called Reuel in the Bible). He was a Midianite priest. Though the land of Midian lay far to the east, its nomadic clans roamed far afield in search of pasture, and they were a familiar sight in the Sinai peninsula.

When Jethro asked his daughters why they had returned sooner than usual, they gave him a bubbling report of the kind "Egyptian" they had met. "And where is he?" asked Jethro. "Why have you left the man? Call him, that he may eat bread" (Exodus 2:20). Moses was invited to stay at their encampment, and he did so. In the course of time, he married Jethro's daughter, Zipporah.

FROM PALACE TO TENT

What a startling change it was in his fortunes to be thrust so abruptly from royal luxury into primitive life with this Bedouin family! But Moses seems to have adapted well. His was now a life of simplicity, looking after his father-in-law's flocks, roaming with them

The landscape in the
new life of the young
Moses, raw and
primitive as on the day
of creation. This is
where he wandered,
alone with his thoughts,
and sensed for the first
time the guiding spirit
controlling the powerful
and mysterious elements
of nature.

43

over the desert in search of occasional scrub, watering them, at times sleeping under the heavens, at times returning to the encampment at night, chatting with the wise old Jethro and the other men of the clan round the camp fire, listening to their legends and the stories of their lives and wanderings, absorbing the lore of the desert. From their tales and from his own day-to-day experiences in the wilderness, he became a "man of the desert", with an intimate knowledge of the terrain, alive to its many dangers, alert to what modest blessings it offered, familiar with its moods in each season. Like the knowledge he had acquired as a prince at the court of the emperor, this knowledge, too, would prove of decisive value to him in later years.

Life in the desert gave him something else, of far deeper significance. For the first time, he was in close and continuous touch with nature, in all its variety. It could be grim and bleak. And it could be grand and wondrous, like the blood-red sky at dawn, the star-studded cover of night, the vast emptiness, the seemingly endless stretch of burning sand

— and then the sudden miracle of water. This was all new to Moses, and it was a strange experience. The drama of nature was taken for granted by the accustomed Bedouin, born and brought up in the desert. It was accepted almost without reflection as normal and familiar. Moses could only wonder — and think.

He thought much as he wandered, alone with his flocks, day after day across the expanse of Sinai. The elements of nature were powerful and mysterious, and they were clearly controlled by a guiding hand. The guidance must come from that invisible God of whom his sister Miriam had spoken at their secret talks in the palace. At that time, however, he had been a prince, surrounded by temple priests and the worship of Egyptian gods, and he had found it hard to grasp the unusual notion of an all-powerful divinity who could neither be touched nor seen. Now, after years of silent, lonely contact with the marvels of creation, he could understand in full measure the strange concept which had baffled him in his pagan youth.

44

Struggling crops in the land of Goshen, where the Israelite tribes dwelt. As State slaves, they could work their land only during the brief intervals between long spells of forced labor.

THE BURNING BUSH

It was in this mood that, while grazing his flocks near Mount Horeb (Mount Sinai) one day, he chanced upon a burning bush. He was startled because the bush went on burning but "it was not consumed" (Exodus 3:2). Curious to see why, he approached it; but he suddenly stopped in his tracks as out of the fiery bush came the voice of God, "the God of your father, the God of Abraham... of Isaac, and ... of Jacob", the names of his ancestors which had been whispered to him by Miriam. "Moses, Moses", cried the voice, and he replied, "Here am I". "Put off your shoes from your feet, for the place on which you are standing is holy ground" (Exodus 3:4–6).

God then told Moses that he had "seen the affliction of my people who are in Egypt" and would now come to their rescue. He would deliver them out of the hand of the Egyptians and bring them to the Promised Land, in fulfillment of his Covenant with the Hebrew Patriarchs. The human instrument who would "bring forth my people, the sons of Israel, out of Egypt", freeing them from slavery and launching them on the road to independent

45

Foreign chieftains
subject to Egyptian rule
bring tribute to the
Pharaoh. A wall
painting in a 15th
century BC tomb in
Thebes, the ancient
capital of Upper Egypt.

47

The Lord said to Aaron, 'Go into the wilderness to meet Moses.' So he went, and met him at the mountain of God and kissed him (Exodus 4:27)

The brothers Moses and Aaron. From
a painting on wood in the Byzantine
Monastery of St. Catherine in
southern Sinai.

religious and national life, would be — Moses.

In a flash, everything must have fallen into place in Moses' mind. There had clearly been a specific purpose to the apparently chance and random events in his past. He had meditated day and night throughout his desert years upon the strange ups and downs and queer twists of fortune which had marked his life, wondering what to make of them. He had turned them over in his mind, rather like the rotation of a mental kaleidoscope, and, in an instant, the revelation at Mount Horeb had produced a clear design, full of meaning. His rescue from the Nile as a baby, his royal upbringing, the talks with his sister Miriam (and perhaps with other members of his family), the sight of his suffering and enslaved people, the killing of the Egyptian overseer, his escape, his years in the wilderness — all suddenly made sense. Each episode had had its purpose, and the overall purpose had just been revealed by the divine voice from the flaming bush. His entire life up to this moment had been a preparation for his role of destiny.

And he was ready for it, though he showed an initial reluctance. He spoke of his faults —

perhaps looking for reassurance. He was not the right man, he said. God brushed aside his hesitations. He was "slow of speech and of tongue". Never mind, replied the Lord; his eloquent brother, Aaron, would be his spokesman. But what if the people would not accept him as their leader, nor believe in his divine mission? For answer, God gave him "signs". He turned Moses' rod into a serpent and back again into a rod. He made his hand leprous and instantly cured it. Using the rod, Moses would "do the signs" (Exodus 4:17) when he reached Egypt, and this would convince the people that "the Lord, the God of their fathers... has appeared to you".

The words of God ceased. The desert was silent. Moses stood awhile, filled with awe, pondering on the mighty but exalted task that lay before him. He had been given the goal — the salvation of his people. Henceforth, without doubt or hesitation, guided by God, he would move firmly towards it.

49

Moses and Aaron went to Pharaoh and said, 'Thus says the Lord, the God of Israel, Let my people go...'

(Exodus 5:1)

Moses, with Aaron, demanding of the Pharaoh (left), that he "let my people go". When he refused, Egypt suffered its first plague, as the waters of the Nile were turned to blood (right). Both illustrations are in the 14th century Golden Haggadah from Spain.

the locusts came up over all the land of Egypt...they ate all the plants...and all the fruit of the trees

(Exodus 10:14, 15)

Close-up of locusts. A swarm of locusts can descend upon a field of ripe corn and devour it in minutes. In the eighth plague, they came in such numbers that they darkened the skies and settled on every plant.

CHAPTER 4 THE RESISTANCE LEADER

*In which Moses returns to Egypt and startles
the Israelite elders at a dramatic assembly.*

As he turned slowly homewards, moving gently with his animals back to his father-in-law's encampment, Moses had time to think of the immediate problems that lay before him. The first was having to tell Jethro that he was leaving. It would be hard for both of them, for the two had become close friends in the years they had been together, and each had developed a respect and a warm admiration for the other, But Moses was confident that his wise and gracious, father-in-law, would understand, and would even help with arrangements for his journey. His real problems would begin once he set foot inside Egypt. One, however, had already been disposed of. He had been troubled by the thought that as soon as he reached Egypt, he might be arrested as a "wanted" man for the incident which had forced him to escape some years earlier, and his mission would end in failure before it began. On this he had been reassured by the Lord. The incident was now forgotten, and "all the men who were seeking your life are dead" (Exodus 4:19).

His major task upon arrival in Egypt would be to get in touch with his own people,

straighten their backs, organize them into a compact group and rally them with the cry of freedom. He would need to infuse them with such faith in this dangerous but divine venture that they would break their shackles of slavery and follow him out of Egypt. He may well have thought, as he wandered back to his desert camp after his encounter at the burning bush, that this might prove the toughest obstacle he would have to hurdle — more difficult even than getting to see the Pharaoh and moving him to set free his Hebrew bondsmen. How could he persuade the Israelites to see him, let alone listen to him? After all, if the Egyptian authorities had forgotten him, his people would have forgotten him too. If he suddenly appeared in their midst, a man of the desert, and told them his fantastic story, and why he had come and what he expected of them, they would ridicule him as a sun-crazed Bedouin nomad, more to be pitied than obeyed.

However, he was encouraged by the knowledge that the path to his people would be smoothed by his brother Aaron. This we know from the Bible, which records that God

The Israelites left Egypt in such haste that they had to take "their dough before it was leavened". There are parts of Sinai where unleavened bread is still baked in the same way. The dough (flour and water) is kneaded (above), a pit prepared, and glowing charcoal placed at the bottom. The rolled dough is spread over the charcoal and covered by another layer of charcoal (below). It is then left to bake. After a short while, the unleavened bread is ready (right) and is removed from the pit.

told Moses: "Aaron, your brother, the Levite... is coming out to meet you" (Exodus 4:14). What is not reported in the Bible, but which seems highly probable, is that Moses had kept in periodic touch with his family during the years he spent in the desert. Through trusted messengers from Jethro's clan, he had very likely managed to get word through to his relatives, shortly after his flight from Egypt, that he was alive and well. Since then, there had no doubt been further exchanges of messages between them. And now he had been advised that Aaron would be meeting him somewhere along the route. Aaron would thus accompany Moses back to Egypt, and he would introduce him to their people. Since Aaron was clearly a distinguished member of the much respected tribe of Levi, his sponsorship would guarantee Moses a sympathetic hearing.

By the time Moses reached the encampment with his flock, his course was clear. He took Jethro aside and told him that he had to return to Egypt. It is evident from the Bible that he said nothing of his experience at the burning bush and nothing of his inspired

it was not leavened, because they… could not tarry…
(Exodus 12:39)

This month [Nissan] shall be for you the beginning of months *(Exodus 12:2)*

The Hebrew letters, bottom left, spell Nissan, the
Hebrew month in which the Festival of Passover is
celebrated. Nissan is also the first month of spring,
which is represented in the lower half of this detail of
the well-preserved mosaic of the Zodiac circle. It
was discovered in the early 4th century synagogue
of Hamat-Tiberias on the Sea of Galilee.

mission. The simple reason he gave was the
wish to see his family after he had been away
so long. "Let me go back, I pray, to my
kinsmen in Egypt and see whether they are
still alive" (Exodus 4:18). Jethro must have
felt for some time that Moses was bound to
leave him one day. After so exciting an early
life, this bright young man would not wish to
end his days as a desert shepherd. He would be
roused by the longing to return to a more
active and stimulating pattern of living. He
was apparently roused now, and Jethro saw
no point in trying to persuade him to stay.
All he said to Moses was: "Go in peace". And
so Moses took leave of his father-in-law and
the clan. He set his wife, Zipporah, and his
two sons, Gershom and Eliezer, upon a
donkey, and they made their way towards
Egypt.

THE BROTHERS MEET

The meeting with Aaron took place along the
way, and we can imagine what an emotional
meeting that must have been. But Moses must
have been too full of his mission to spend
much time on celebrating their reunion. He

had news of mighty importance to impart to
his brother and much serious business to
discuss. Aaron would be his principal as-
sistant and spokesman throughout all the
struggles that lay ahead, and he had to be
"brought up to date" without delay. He had
to be given details of the dramatic revelation
at the burning bush and of the divine goal
that had been set, and the two brothers had
to work out the best way to go about their
gigantic task. Accordingly, at this wayside
desert meeting, "Moses told Aaron all the
words of the Lord with which he had sent him,
and all the signs which he had charged him to
do" (Exodus 4:28). Aaron's first job would be
to arrange for Moses to meet the representatives of their community, and to pave the way
for their acceptance of Moses' authority.

The Bible tells us little of how the Hebrews
in Egypt at that time were organized and
how they ran their communal affairs. It is
clear, however, that the basic framework of
the community was the tribe, and the tribe
was composed of a number of clans. The clan
was really a family in its widest sense, which

...with unleavened bread and bitter herbs they shall eat it. ...It is the Lord's passover *(Exodus 12:8, 11)*

The Seder service on the first night of Passover is celebrated in Jewish homes throughout the world. All recite the Haggadah, with its story of the Exodus, commentaries and songs; and all say the same prayers and serve the same symbolic dishes. This family, conducting the Seder in Jerusalem, came from Yemen.

included not simply parents and children but uncles and aunts and cousins and even more distant relatives. Each clan would have its head, and it was probably the clan leaders who chose one of their number to be the head of the tribe. On any major decision affecting the tribe, the tribal leader would no doubt consult with the clan leaders. Decisions affecting the entire community would probably be reached at a meeting of the tribal leaders. This, then, was the organizational framework in which Moses and Aaron would work.

One factor which would make their work easier was that the people were not scattered throughout the country. They all lived in and around the land of Goshen. They were the descendants of the first settlers of this region, Jacob and his sons, the founders of the tribes of Israel, and all belonged to one or other of these tribes.

It is likely that though the community was in bondage, and the status of each individual was therefore that of a State slave, they were not necessarily engaged in slave labor all the time. But they could be; for the authorities had the power to call upon the community *at*

The scene on Mount Gerizim on the first night of the Samaritan Passover. The Samaritans have a curious history. When the Assyrians conquered Samaria (the northern Kingdom of Israel) in the 8th century BC, they brought in people from other lands which they had overrun. The relatively few Israelites who remained merged with these people, and their descendants were known as Samaritans (that is, from Samaria). They followed a form of Judaism in which only the Five Books of Moses (the Torah) were accepted as sacred scripture. Mount Gerizim in Samaria was considered holy, and there they assemble on Passover eve, and follow literally the Torah instruction to sacrifice the paschal lamb and eat it in haste.

all times to provide laborers without pay for whatever task they wished. They could take all the males of the community for slave labor for long periods, or they might take only a few for short periods. They could put them on tough physical labor or let them off with only light work. They could give them ample notice or seize them without warning. It all depended on the whim of the Pharaoh and on his attitude towards the Hebrews. A Pharaoh who hated them might issue an order for all male Hebrew to be rounded up and kept permanently on hard labor. During the reign of a less harsh ruler, the Israelites would have more time at home to spend with their families, to cultivate their fields and graze their flocks. When they were taken off on forced labor, their wives and children would have to manage as best they could.

A CALL TO REVOLT

The Pharaohs in the time of Moses, first Sethos I and then Rameses II, were harsh rulers, and the Hebrews had been subjected to prolonged and cruel suffering. To free them, Moses had to secure their trust and support, and the first obvious step was to gain acceptance by the tribal leaders. Their endorsement would ensure popular backing for his mission of rescue. And so "Moses and Aaron went and gathered all the elders of the people of Israel", and at this crucial first meeting, upon which so much depended, "Aaron spoke all the words which the Lord had spoken to Moses, and did the signs in the sight of the people" (Exodus 4:29, 30).

Behind these brief biblical phrases lies the drama of what must have happened at this first encounter. Aaron, with Moses at his side, tried to rouse the tribal leaders with a startling appeal — which was nothing less than a call to revolt against the Egyptian tyrant and make themselves free. Their situation, Aaron told them, and as they well knew, was dreadful. They had struck rock bottom. Worst of all, they were without hope. They accepted their misfortune as a natural disaster. Well, said Aaron, he had come to announce the stupendous news that their days of slavery were about to end. God had told Moses that he had not forgotten his people. Nor had he forgotten his promise to

The stained glass
windows by Marc
Chagall in the synagogue
at the Hadassah-Hebrew
University Medical
Center in Jerusalem. The
twelve window paintings
depict the characteristics
of the tribes of Israel as
described in the Bible.

63

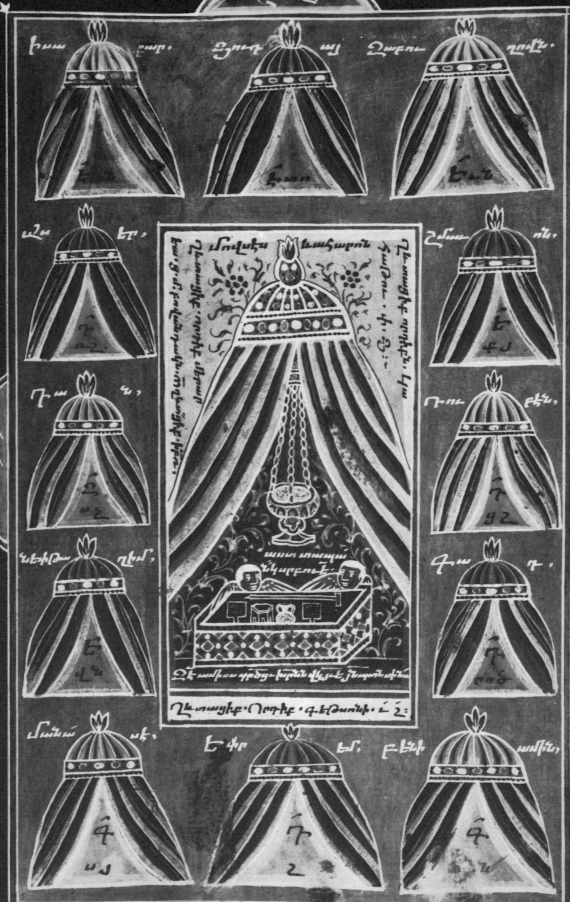

The twelve tribes, represented by tents, grouped round the Tabernacle containing the Ark of the Covenant, as imagined by a 17th century artist. An illustration from a manuscript in the Library of St. Thoros, attached to the Armenian Orthodox Patriarchate, Jerusalem.

their forefathers, the Patriarchs Abraham, Isaac and Jacob. He had seen their sufferings and had decided to set them on the road to freedom. The moment of salvation had arrived.

Aaron was eloquent and persuasive. The towering figure of the silent Moses may well have been impressive. But it is most probable that they failed to sway the sceptical and down-to-earth tribal leaders. Their doubts would have been echoed in their pointed questions. It was all very well for Aaron to say that God had spoken to Moses; but had he also spoken to Pharaoh? What were they now expected to do? Calmly tell their Egyptian taskmasters that they no longer felt themselves slaves and would not be reporting for work in the morning? In the grim practical world in which they lived, they knew that if they did this, their ringleaders would be promptly executed and the rest would be beaten and shackled. Did Aaron think their lives would be saved if they explained that they were acting according to the will of God? Who would believe them? And even if they were believed, which Egyptian official would

pay the slightest attention to the will of the Hebrew God? Some of the tribal leaders may have gone further and asked why they, the elders of the community, should believe all that Aaron had told them?

It was no doubt at this point that Aaron "did the signs", performing the miracles that had been displayed to Moses in the desert beside the burning bush. This must have reassured the leaders that Moses and Aaron were indeed divine messengers, and that what they had heard was indeed the word of God. They were now ready to listen to the two brothers and learn what steps they proposed to take.

THE PEOPLE RESPOND

Moses and Aaron outlined their course of action. The immediate aim was a general uprising, turning the entire Israelite community into members of a resistance movement. However, the object was not to overthrow the existing Pharaoh or his regime. That was beyond their scope and capability. But above all it was not necessary. For the intention was not to make Egypt a land in

65

The hot springs at Hamam Far'aoun on the east bank of the Gulf of Suez and the western edge of the Sinai desert. The name is Arabic for "the hot waters of Pharaoh". According to local legend, this is where the Egyptian chariots pursuing the Israelites got stuck, and Pharaoh's hot fury raised the temperature of the water.

67

which the Hebrews might continue to live
without suffering. The purpose was to take
the Hebrews out of Egypt and bring them to
their own promised land where they could
create and be masters of their own religious
and national life.

Moses and Aaron may have painted a rosy
picture of what life would be like for free men
in their own land. But they left their listeners
with no illusions about the hardships, dif-
ficulties and dangers they would experience
before getting there. One danger, however,
would be avoided. They would not, at first,
call upon the slaves to turn on their masters.
The Hebrews were too weak and Egypt was
too mighty. The rebellion would be crushed
quickly, and it might be followed by the
slaughter of the entire community. No. What
needed to be done was to bring about a
change of heart in the Pharaoh, so that he
himself would find it in the interests of his
country to free the Hebrew slaves and allow
them to leave. Persuading the Pharaoh to
adopt this revolutionary policy would be the
task of Moses, guided in all his actions by
the Lord.

This meeting with the tribal leaders was a
success. They responded to Moses' call. But
they were evidently doubtful whether they
alone could convince their people, and they
must have asked Moses and Aaron to appear
with them at a mass gathering and repeat
their "signs". They themselves had been won
over when they had witnessed the wonders
performed by Aaron, and what had impressed
them would surely impress the general
public. We can assume that this is what must
have happened at this vital meeting with the
elders of the community, for immediately
afterwards, as we learn from the Bible, Aaron
"did the signs in the sight of the people." The
response was instant and unanimous. "And
the people believed; and when they heard that
the Lord had visited the people of Israel and
that he had seen their affliction, they bowed
their heads and worshipped" (Exodus 4:31).

The Egyptians pursued them, all Pharaoh's horses a

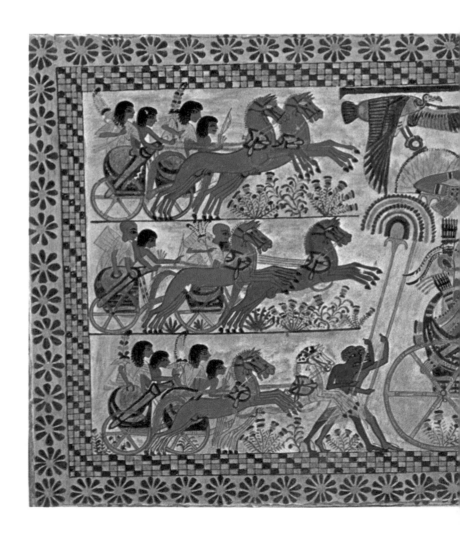

Pharaoh's chariot. This is a detail
from a 14th century BC painting on
a wooden chest discovered in the
tomb of Tutankhamun at Thebes.

...ariots...and overtook them...at the sea (Exodus 14:9)

the people of Israel went into the midst of the sea on dry ground…the Lord said to Moses, 'Stretch out your hand over the sea…' The waters returned and covered the chariots and…the host of Pharaoh (*Exodus 14:22, 26, 28*)

Two illustrations in a 1601 Armenian hymn book in the library of St. Thoros, Jerusalem. The one on the right shows the Israelites reaching dry land after the waters had parted. On the left, the luckless Egyptian troops are caught by the returning seas. The artist has linked the two scenes with the staff of Moses.

CHAPTER 5 THE ROYAL MEETING

*In which a furious king turns down a request by
Moses, but catastrophe changes the monarch's mind.*

Armed with the support of the community, Moses and Aaron could now take their next decisive step: the approach to the Pharaoh. But how did they gain entry to the palace, let alone get to see the ruler himself? The Bible does not tell us, recording simply that "Moses and Aaron went to Pharaoh and said...". But even in the modern world, it is not any-body who can walk into Buckingham Palace and ask to see the Queen, or enter the White House or the Kremlin and get taken straight to the President. How, then, did the two Hebrew brothers manage to gain an audience with the even more unapproachable Egyptian monarch of the 13th century BC? Scholars have put forward several theories. Some suggest that one of the boyhood court com-panions of Moses, or a surviving palace official who had known him as a lad, may have arranged it. Others think it possible that the princess, Moses' foster mother, may still have been alive, and, helpful as ever, used her influence with the king.

Perhaps, however, Moses and his brother were able to reach the royal presence in a much simpler way. Among the ancient Egyptian documents which have come to light, there is one which dates back to the reign of Rameses II, the very Pharaoh whom Moses was about to meet. In this document, the writer described the delights of living in the restored town of Avaris. This, it will be recalled, was the ancient capital of the Hyksos which Rameses had reconstructed with the labor of the Hebrew slaves and renamed Raamses. In his account, the scribe wrote: "Oh, the joy of dwelling there.... No wish is unfulfilled: the humble man and the mighty are as one...all men equally can lay their request before him [Pharaoh]." Of course, we must discount the obvious exaggeration in such writings, which were meant to present the king in the most favorable light. But it seems that in order to demonstrate his popularity, the Pharaoh, as a token gesture, held an occasional "open house" to which any member of the public could come with a plea. It may be, therefore, that all Moses had to do was appear at the palace on one such occasion and join the queue of suppliants waiting to be admitted to the throne room.

But however the audience was contrived,

the moment came when Moses and Aaron found themselves face to face with the Pharaoh. He must have been very surprised by their manner, for, though the biblical record is brief, it is clear that the two Hebrews showed no sense of dread and none of veneration in the presence of the mighty ruler. They did not come to beg, and they did not grovel at the master's feet. Armed with the guidance of the Lord, they entered with heads erect, and they spoke with confidence. At this first meeting, they did not raise the central issue of freeing the slaves. As a tactful opening, they simply asked the Pharaoh's permission to let them pray and worship their God at a place "three days' journey into the wilderness". "Thus says the Lord, the God of Israel," they told the ruler. "Let my people go, that they may hold a feast for me in the wilderness" (Exodus 5:1).

THE KING'S REVENGE

The king's reaction was to be expected. He was outraged. For one thing, he was not used to receiving people who wore such an air of confidence and who spoke to him almost as equal to equal. It was more usual for his subjects, whether lowborn or noblemen, to abase themselves before him. As for their request, it was unheard of for slaves to be given an extended holiday. The very idea was absurd. Indeed, if he were mad enough to grant it, he would be setting a dangerous precedent. Other slave groups would make demands for similar privileges, and where would it all end? One privilege would lead to another, and before long there would be no more slavery, and the whole economic and social system of the country would be upset. And what a ridiculous excuse his two visitors had put forward for the Hebrews to get leave from their labors: to worship "their God" in the wilderness! "Who is the Lord," he said "that I should heed his voice and let Israel go?" (Exodus 5:2).

As soon as Moses and Aaron were dimissed, the Pharaoh gave orders for the work load of the Hebrew slaves to be increased. Their daily quota of brick-making was to remain, but now, instead of being provided with the raw materials, they would have to scurry around and find their own. This would teach them

74

to remember who and what they were, and what to expect if they were ever again moved to be so impudent. It would also, as he cunningly expected, set the slaves against their leaders.

He was right. They were furious. And their anger over their added burdens was directed not at their Egyptian taskmasters but against Moses. He had come to them with magic words and the promise of freedom, and here they were overloaded with even "heavier work" than before, and whipped into the bargain to hurry them up. "The Lord look upon you and judge," they shouted to Moses and Aaron with deep bitterness, "because you have made us offensive in the sight of Pharaoh and his servants, and have put a sword in their hands to kill us" (Exodus 5:21).

Thus was the first major resistance movement in recorded history faced with a key problem which would be met by every subsequent movement to resist oppression, right down to our own day: how to rouse a people to overcome their fear of reprisal and take action against a tyrant. It is fear of what the tyrant will do to them that keeps them passive. This is very understandable. It is never a light matter — and it certainly was not in the Egypt of those days — for the weak and unarmed to defy oppressive authority. But a few sturdy souls can set the example, and by so doing can release the pent-up feelings of a persecuted community and launch a successful revolt.

Moses understood this instinctively. And he also knew, after Pharaoh's punishment, that he needed to implant in his people the will to resist. This would have been a hard task even if the circumstances were ideal. It was particularly difficult for Moses since he had to deal with a loosely organized community whose senses had been dulled and their spirit crushed by years of enslavement. He had to educate them anew, and he started with the leading men of the tribes and clans. He and Aaron spent countless hours with them trying to breathe life into their despondent souls, change their outlook, give them hope, ideals and new horizons. They did so without minimizing the risks and the sufferings. The struggle would be long and full of peril. There would be casualties. But if they held firm, and had confidence in themselves, they would gain the exalted goal. Moses was able to win them over — as earlier he had gained their acceptance of him as leader — primarily through their faith in God, the God of their Patriarchs. He had abandoned them — but he had now remembered them. And there was a persuasive conviction behind Moses' words because he himself believed so deeply in God and in the fulfillment of God's promise. Not all revolts have been successful, and not every resistance leader has been free of doubt. But Moses, moved by the spirit of God, at no time doubted that the mission of liberation would succeed.

"LET MY PEOPLE GO"

Now that the tribal elders were more solidly behind him, Moses could move on to the next phase of his resistance campaign. He was mature enough, and he had had enough experience as a youth at court, to realize that no Egyptian ruler would free his slaves upon request. No man of power ever gives up power willingly. He does so only when he is compelled to, either by armed force, in a dictatorship, or, in a democracy, by an adverse vote. But whatever the regime, it may be prepared to give up certain pockets of power when holding on to that power becomes a liability. (A good example of this in our generation is the reluctant grant of independence by Britain, France and Belgium to their African colonies.)

Circumstances had to be created which would make the Pharaoh recognize that the Hebrew slaves had become a liability to himself and to his country, that keeping them would bring him damage, and that it would be in his interest to heed Moses' demand that he "let my people go". These circumstances were provided by the Lord — in the form of the Ten Plagues. As each became insufferable, the Pharaoh agreed to let the Israelites leave. But as each affliction was lifted, he changed his mind. "I will harden Pharaoh's heart", said the Lord, to reassure Moses at the king's successive betrayals. The object was to build up a mounting impact upon the emperor as plague followed plague which would make him welcome the departure of the Hebrews.

First, the waters of the Nile were turned to

The oasis of Kadesh Barnea, which the Israelites were to reach two years after leaving Egypt.

blood. Then came the frogs. Then gnats, attacking man and beast. Then swarms of flies. This was followed by a plague on Egyptian cattle; an epidemic of boils; a fierce hailstorm; clouds of locusts which devoured all the crops; and then a three-day spell of utter darkness.

These natural disasters, divinely decreed, were carefully chosen. They were aimed to strike at the very center of the Pharaoh's power. Each Pharaoh believed, and wished his people to believe, that he was selected by the gods, and was in fact god-like. This was the condition of his authority — and of the well-being of the country. It was the general opinion that if he were the true choice of the gods, then the land would be blessed with prosperity. Crops would be plentiful, flocks would multiply, and the people would live at peace with each other. If, however, the Pharaoh was not what he claimed to be — was not in fact chosen by the Egyptian deities — then the country would be struck by catastrophe.

Thus, the plagues which now afflicted the land, polluting the Nile, destroying the crops, killing the flocks, bringing starvation and misery, were the disasters most likely to make people doubt the divine choice of the Pharaoh. It was this more than anything else, more than a concern for his people's sufferings, that was calculated to move the Pharaoh to allow the Hebrews to leave and thereby put an end to catastrophe; for it endangered the very basis of his authority.

THE FIRST PASSOVER

The final calamity, however, the tenth and harshest of all, brought deep personal suffering to the Pharaoh too. This was the death of the first-born in every Egyptian family, high and low. It was timed for the night of the fourteenth of the Hebrew month of Nissan, and the Lord told Moses and Aaron to prepare the Israelites for that night, and for their immediate exodus from Egypt.

Four days before, every Israelite family was to bring home a lamb or a kid. On the evening of the fourteenth, it was to be slaughtered, and some of its blood smeared on the doorposts and lintel of each house. This sign would mark off the Hebrew homes, and they would be passed over when the Lord came to smite the Egyptians. The animal was to be roasted and eaten hurriedly that night so little time would be lost in setting out on the long journey. "In this manner shall you eat it: your loins girded, your sandals on your feet, and your staff in your hand; and you shall eat it in haste. It is the Lord's passover" (Exodus 12:11).

At midnight the Lord struck, and the first-born sons of all the Egyptians died. A great cry went up in the land, and that same night the Pharaoh summoned Moses and Aaron and announced his surrender: the Hebrew slaves could leave. "Rise up, go forth from among my people, both you and the people of Israel; and go, serve the Lord, as you have said. Take your flocks and your herds...and be gone; and bless me also!" (Exodus 12:31, 32). The Egyptian people also urged the Hebrews to hurry out. To speed their departure, they gave them jewels and other valuables. It was the first time the slaves had received anything from the Egyptians — other than blows to make them work harder. They left, setting out in a southeasterly direction for

When Pharaoh let the people go, God did not lead them by way of the land of the Philistines, although that was near (Exodus 13:17)

The narrow "Way of the Sea" or "Way of the Land of the Philistines", which ran along the Mediterranean at the northern edge of Sinai. It was used by commercial caravans and imperial armies, and the Bible says that the Israelites did not take this route. A few scholars, however, hold that they started off along it, and soon turned south into the desert. The photograph shows the remains of ancient fortifications which guarded this highway.

The oasis of Wadi Firan.
This is believed to be the
site of biblical Elim,
well-watered and thick
with palm and tamarisk,
which so refreshed the
Israelites after their
disappointment at Marah.

82

Sinai. They had taken their first step along the road to freedom.

God had told Moses: "This day shall be for you a memorial day... throughout your generations you shall observe it as an ordinance for ever" (Exodus 12:14). To this day, Jews throughout the world celebrate the spring Festival of Passover to commemorate the Exodus. It is the great Jewish festival of freedom. On the first night there is a ritual meal, called the Seder. (In Israel there is only one Seder and the festival lasts seven days. In other countries, Jews repeat the Seder on the second night and celebrate the festival for eight days.) The Seder is held at home and all members of the family participate. They read the Haggadah, which tells the story of the Exodus, and they taste special foods which symbolize the dramatic events of that liberation. They eat *matza* (throughout the entire festival) to remind them of the hasty departure of their ancestors. *Matza* is flat, unleavened bread, rather like large crackers, and the Israelites left Egypt so hurriedly that the bread they baked that day had no time to rise. "So the people took their dough before it was leavened" (Exodus 12:34). They eat bitter herbs at the Seder to recall the bitterness of Israelite slavery in Egypt. And they place a bone on the table to represent the paschal lamb whose blood was daubed on the Israelite dwellings which God passed over when he plagued the Egyptians. Four goblets of wine are drunk during the recital of the Exodus story, possibly to mark the four biblical terms used by God in his promise to free the Israelites: "I will bring you out from under the burdens of the Egyptians...deliver you...redeem you...and I will take you.." (Exodus 6:6, 7). Perhaps the most impressive, educational and relevant passage in the Haggadah is the one which begins: "Every Jew in every generation should feel as if he himself came out of Egypt." It points to the key purpose of the Passover festival, the occasion when every Jew can personally identify with these happenings in his people's past, and as if he himself were an Israelite launching himself into freedom.

CHAPTER 6 THE WATERS PART

In which the king changes his mind again, and his pursuing chariots trap the Israelite slaves with their backs to the sea.

Clan by clan and tribe by tribe, the Hebrews with their flocks began their great trek. Their first stop was a place called Succoth, just west of today's Ismailia on the Suez Canal. From there they went on to Etham, "on the edge of the wilderness". To lead them along the way, "the Lord went before them by day in a pillar of cloud... and by night in a pillar of fire" (Exodus 13:21). They then moved off towards the Reed Sea and put up their tents on its western shore. [The English version of the Bible calls it the "Red Sea" (Exodus 13:18), but this is a mistranslation of the Hebrew *Yam-Suf.* (Hebrew was the original language of the Bible.) *Yam* is Hebrew for "sea" and *Suf* means "reed", so the correct translation is "Sea of Reeds". It was clearly very close to the Egyptian-North Sinai border, as the Israelites had departed only a little while earlier, and should not be confused with what is known today as the Red Sea, the large body of water which lies to the south of the southernmost tip of the Sinai Peninsula. We shall be considering the probable location of the Reed Sea later.]

Here, at the water's edge, the Israelites were to suffer their first frightening experience — and enjoy one of their greatest triumphs.

It took several days for the Egyptians to start recovering from the series of disasters which had suddenly struck them. Their first-born had been buried, the Nile was no longer red, the air was free of gnats and flies, and life was beginning to return to normal. One feature alone was missing from the Egyptian scene: the Israelite slaves. The Pharaoh and his advisers were no longer under the pressure of catastrophe, and they could now think over quietly and calmly the events of the previous weeks. The more they thought of those terrible happenings, which had ended with the departure of the Hebrews, the more furious they became. Had they been tricked? Could the "God" of whom Moses and Aaron had spoken really have been responsible for the ten plagues? Most of them, after all, were in the class of natural calamities which Egypt had known from time to time. True, they had never struck all at once, with one following on the heels of another; but nature could be like that.

As the Pharaoh and his counselors con-

they moved on from Succoth, and encamped at Etham

(Exodus 13:20)

"I made the people of Israel dwell in booths when I brought them out of the land of Egypt" (Leviticus 23:43). The booths of a tribal settlement in northern Sinai today.

tinued to study the matter, they convinced themselves that they had been the victims of a gigantic hoax. Those two fellows Moses and Aaron had fooled them. They had seized on natural disasters and turned them to their own advantage, claiming that these punishments had been inflicted by "their God". As a result, Egypt had lost a good part of its slave labor force. This was a hard loss in itself. What was even more grave, however, was the effect it might have on the other forced-labor groups. Hearing of the success of the Hebrews, they might also take it into their heads to revolt and depart. Immediate action was called for. It was essential to go after the Hebrews, bring them back, execute the leaders and deal out suitable punishment to the rest of the rebellious community. This would serve as a dramatic example to their slave communities who might take it into their heads to mutiny. It would also hearten the Egyptian population who had suffered so badly in the plagues.

THE CHASE

The Pharaoh accordingly "made ready his chariot", mobilized his army, "and took six hundred picked chariots and all the other chariots of Egypt with officers over all of them" (Exodus 14:7), and set off in pursuit of the Hebrews. Though he was starting out several days later, the king, with his swift mobile forces, would soon overtake his slow-moving former bondsmen. He caught up with them near the Reed Sea.

When the Israelites saw the Egyptians coming, they were terrified, and Moses faced his first major leadership crisis. The Bible tells us that they cried to Moses: "Is it because there are no graves in Egypt that you have taken us away to die in the wilderness?" (Exodus 14:11). We can imagine the scene. There were the Israelites, an unarmed group of men, women and children, sprawled out with their flocks on the shore, frozen with alarm as they caught sight in the distance of the dust clouds thrown up by the huge army of charioteers charging towards them. With their backs to the water, they were trapped. There was no escape. They would all be killed. In their terror, some of them turned upon Moses. It was all his fault. He had come with his fine

A tree trunk almost as old as time in Wadi Firan, the oasis through which the Israelites passed on their way to Mount Sinai.

talk of freedom, and this was now the situation to which he had brought them — between the Egyptian devil and the sea! Why couldn't he have left them alone? Why couldn't he have let them stay in Egypt? True they would still be slaves; but at least they would be alive. Now they faced slaughter, or drowning.

There is a hint in the next sentence in the Bible that Moses had not found it easy to rouse them against their taskmasters and follow him. For one of the arguments they now used against him was: "Is not this what we said to you in Egypt, 'Let us alone and let us serve the Egyptians'?" (Exodus 14:12). As with every setback in any resistance movement, there would be a good deal of grumbling and murmuring and downright rebellion on the part of the doubters and the weak in faith before the great march to freedom was over.

Guided by the Lord, Moses now had to exert all his powers of leadership and decision to save the day. He must have shown supreme confidence, quieting their hysteria, calming their fears, assuring them that all would be well, infecting them with his own steady faith

in their destiny. "Fear not", he told his people; "stand firm, and see the salvation of the Lord" (Exodus 14:13).

Night fell. The Egyptian force halted, ready to do battle in the morning. Moses ordered the Israelites to get ready to move. At daybreak, "Moses stretched out his hand over the sea; and the Lord drove the sea back by a strong east wind all night, and made the sea dry land, and the waters were divided" (Exodus 14:21). The Israelites promptly set out across this dry ground. Even the frightened ones among them did not hesitate, feeling that they had nothing to lose. To have remained behind would have put them at the mercy of the Egyptian army.

Shortly afterwards, the pursuing soldiers reached the shore — and saw the fleeing Israelites on the other side. They immediately followed. But the ground, which was firm enough to walk across, proved too soft for the heavy chariots, and it "discomfited the host of the Egyptians, clogging their chariot wheels so that they drove heavily" (Exodus 14:24, 25). Horses and vehicles got bogged down in the mud and stuck. Before they could

89

Jebel Mussa, the "Mount of Moses", in the heart of the rugged range that towers above the southern region of Sinai and marks it off from the north. An early Christian tradition holds this to be the site where Moses received the Commandments.

90

get the wheels free and turn back, "The waters returned and covered the chariots and the horsemen and all the host of Pharaoh that had followed them into the sea." All were drowned. The Israelites were saved.

WHERE DID IT HAPPEN?

Where did this encounter take place? Where is the stretch of water which in biblical times was apparently known as the "Reed Sea"? Various suggestions have been put forward. Each is tied to a particular theory of the entire Exodus route, for no one knows for certain exactly which route the Israelites took across the Sinai desert. This is because we do not know the location of *all* the places mentioned in the Bible through which the Israelites passed, though we know a good many. Scholars who know the Bible and who have also journeyed through Sinai have come up with several ideas. The two most popular ones might be called the theory of the northern route and the theory of the southern route. Both are marked on the accompanying map. There is much to be said for both, for each can find support in the biblical references and

modern archaeological discoveries. But most scholars tend to accept the southern route theory.

According to the "northern" scholars, the Reed Sea was what is now known to us as Lake Bardawil. It lies between Kantara and El Arish from west to east, and between the Mediterranean and the sand dunes of northern Sinai from north to south. It is separated from the Mediterranean by a very narrow strip of land, ranging in width from 100 yards to half a mile. This strip formed part of the great coastal highway which ran from Egypt to Syria in ancient times.

When you look at Lake Bardawil, it seems just like a sea. But if you dived into it you would strike your head on the bottom, for its waters are very shallow. Even today, when great chunks of the land strip have been excavated to allow the Mediterranean to flow into the lake (in order to enrich its stock of fish), it is only a foot and a half deep in parts. In ancient times, when the strip was intact, it must have been much shallower. This lake is also swept by uncommonly strong winds, and at times the shallowest parts are barely cover-

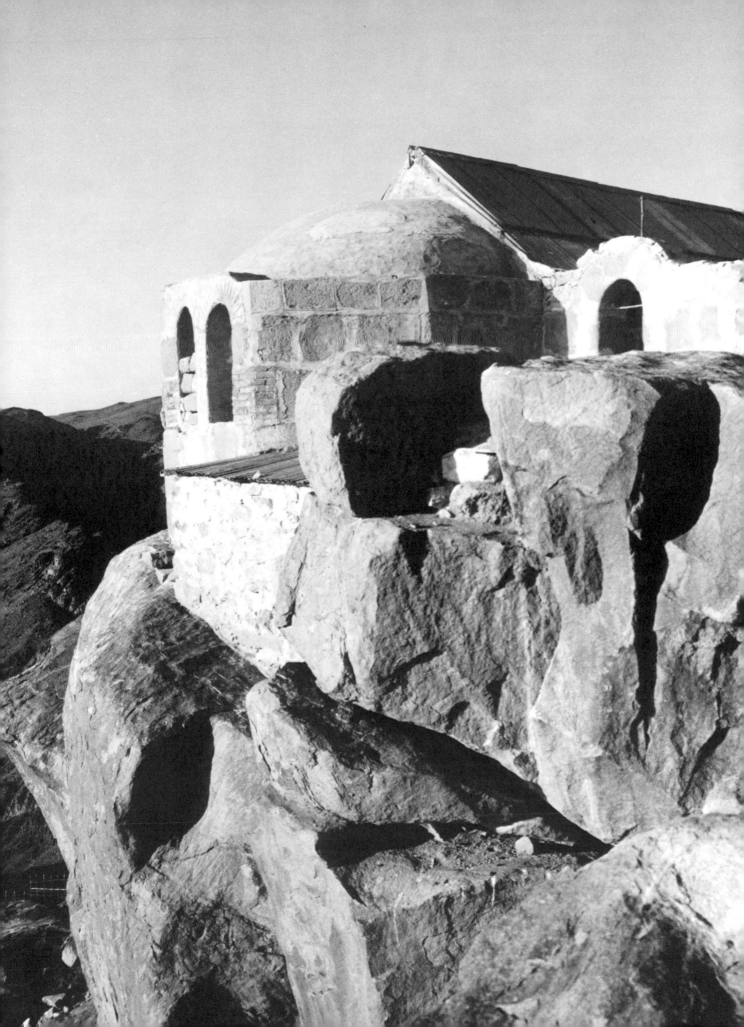

Come up to me on the mountain, and wait there

(Exodus 24:12)

Three thousand steps lead up
to what is sometimes called the
"gateway to heaven", at the
summit of Jebel Mussa.

ed by water. It is therefore suggested that the Israelites may have crossed Bardawil from the narrow northern strip southwards to the sand dunes, and that this would match the biblical account. The Egyptian chariots, coming after them, would have got stuck in the bed of the lake and then, with a change of wind, the waters would have risen and covered them.

From here, according to this theory, the rest of the route through the wilderness would have kept to the northern stretch of the Sinai peninsula. Where, then, would scholars who hold this theory place Mount Sinai? None of them is prepared to say for certain, but some have suggested Jebel Hilel as the possible site. It is a mountain in northeastern Sinai lying to the southwest of Abu Awugeila and Jebel Libne — names made famous in our own day in the Sinai Campaign of 1956 and the Six Day War of 1967. From there, the Israelites would have continued a short distance eastwards to Kadesh Barnea, the large oasis now known as Ain el-Kudeirat, near Kusseima, some fifty miles south of Beersheba. Incidentally, even the "southern" scholars agree that Kadesh Barnea is Ain el-Kudeirat in north-

eastern Sinai, but they claim that the Israelites ended up there only after wandering round southern Sinai.

The "southern" theory would appear to fit the biblical account more smoothly. It is also supported by ancient tradition. Moreover, the Bible says: "When Pharaoh let the people go, God did not lead them by way of the land of the Philistines" — the northern coastal highway — "although that was near; for God said, 'Lest the people repent when they see war, and return to Egypt'" (Exodus 13:17). They would certainly have seen a good deal of war had they taken — and kept to — the northern highway along the Mediterranean coast. For just because it "was near", and the direct route to the Promised Land, it was heavily used by armies and trading caravans — the last people a group of runaway slaves would have wished to meet. The reply of the "northern" theorists is that Moses only started along this northern road, but soon turned southwards across Lake Bardawil. This would have brought him to the area of the dunes, which were impassable to chariots.

St. Catherine's Monastery, set against the mountains of southern Sinai. An early Christian belief that this was the site of the burning bush attracted monks and hermits. The Roman emperor Constantine built a chapel and a refuge tower for them in the 4th century. The emperor Justinian I erected a complete monastery two centuries later, and enclosed the building within a high wall of granite. It looked like a fortress — and still does.

THE BITTER LAKES

However, the "southern" theory holds that the Israelites moved southeast soon after leaving Egypt, and the Reed Sea is identified with the Bitter Lakes. These lie between today's Ismailia and Suez, the port at the head of the Gulf of Suez. The Great Bitter Lake is connected to the more southerly Little Bitter Lake by a strait, and this narrow passage of water is shallow even today. But before the construction of the Suez Canal in the last century, it was quite usual for this strait to become absolutely dry, and easy to walk across. This happened when the water level fell in the Gulf of Suez. When it rose again, the water would begin to seep through the bed of the strait, turning it into mud, and a little while later, there would be a sudden flood. The water would rush through, covering the strait and wiping out the division between the two Bitter Lakes, so that the whole area looked like one large sea.

Many of you may have seen the same kind of thing at seaside resorts in Britain and America. In Britain, particularly along the coast of Cornwall and Devonshire, you visit the coves when the tide is going out, and you see little boats stuck in the mud. When the sun is high, the mud hardens quickly and you can walk perhaps a few hundred yards until you come to the edge of the sea. A few hours later, when the tide comes in, the boats are again bobbing up in the water, and any stranger who had just arrived and knew nothing about tides would never imagine that only shortly before it was possible to walk among the boats without getting one's feet wet.

It seems to me that this occurrence at the strait between the Bitter Lakes well matches the biblical report, and well explains the fear of the Israelites. They had encamped at the edge of the strait without knowing that at this particular locality the water level rose and fell. When they got there towards evening, the level was high, and so the Great Bitter Lake, the Little Bitter Lake and the strait between them looked like one, single, unbroken stretch of water. As far as they were concerned, they were at the edge of a large deep sea which offered no escape from the advancing Egyptian troops. At day break, the level fell, and

The oasis of Ein Furtaga in eastern Sinai. This is a rare photograph of a "sea in the desert". After heavy rains in the distant north, waters rush all the way down to the desert and are briefly trapped in the dry river beds.

99

Drawings scratched on rocks were made by travelers and pilgrims in different historical periods, and are to be found along the caravan routes throughout Sinai. One such rock-drawing was of a menorah, the seven branched candelabrum described in the vision of the prophet Zechariah (4:2). It became the Jewish symbol of the light of the spirit and its supremacy over might. It is today the emblem of the State of Israel.

"the waters were divided" by the now dry strait, the Great Lake on one side and the Little Lake on the other. The Israelites walked across. If the Egyptians had waited a while, the ground might have been hard enough to bear the weight of their vehicles. But they must have been so anxious to catch the Hebrew slaves as soon as they had spotted them that they followed them without delay. Their chariots thus got mired in the mud, and before they could pull them free, the level rose again and the waters rushed through to cover them.

CHAPTER 7 THE LONG MARCH TO FREEDOM

*In which the tribes meet the adventurous challenge
of the desert — and an attack by wild raiders.*

According to the "southern" theory, after crossing between the Bitter Lakes and moving a short distance inland, the Israelites turned south. They journeyed along the eastern shore of the Gulf of Suez, past today's Port Taufiq, Ras Sudar and Abu Rudeis. They then wheeled east into Wadi Firan, and on to Mount Sinai. No scholar is prepared to identify Mount Sinai as today's Jebel Mussa. But an early Christian tradition held that this forbidding peak in the wild and rugged mountain country of southern Sinai was the mountain where Moses received the Ten Commandments. In the 4th century AD — some 17 centuries after the Exodus — Emperor Constantine built a chapel at the foot of a nearby lower slope. It marked what was believed to have been the site of the burning bush. Together with the chapel, Constantine built a refuge tower for hermits. In the 6th century AD, Emperor Justinian I added to it an entire monastery compound, and enclosed it within a high wall of grey granite to give monks protection from marauders. Several centuries later it became known as St. Catherine's Monastery. Today's structure is basically the building of Justinian, and still looks like a fortress.

Whatever the exact location of Mount Sinai, the "southern" theorists think it was certainly somewhere in this mountainous southern region of the Sinai peninsula. By taking this route, the Israelites would have been least likely to meet Egyptian troops. Nor would they have met them when, after receiving the Ten Commandments, they moved through little-traveled tracks until they reached Kadesh Barnea.

The important point to remember with all these theories is that as far as the history of Israel is concerned, any discussion of the Exodus route is only of interest to scholars. For the basic fact remains that no matter where in Sinai the Law-giving ceremony took place, it was that momentous occasion itself which laid the foundations of the Jewish religion and Jewish nationhood.

When the Israelites "saw the Egyptian dead upon the shore" — presumably after the water level had again dropped — they sang a song of thankfulness and glory to the Lord.

We remember the fish we ate in Egypt for nothing
(Numbers 11:5)

A wall painting in an Egyptian tomb belonging to the 13th century BC, the period of the Exodus. It suggests "the fleshpots" of Egypt, which the Israelites longed for during their early months of hunger in the wilderness.

Miriam, sister of Moses, took a timbrel in her hand and led the women in dance. Their spirits were high and their confidence in Moses was restored. But three days later, after trekking through the scorching Wilderness of Shur, they came up against the main problem of all who journey in the desert — water. They arrived at Marah, and found its water too bitter to drink. (Marah is the Hebrew word for bitter.) "And the people murmured against Moses" (Exodus 15:25).

This gentle phrase, "the people murmured", meaning that they complained, crops up often in the biblical story of the Exodus; for throughout their wilderness years they were often full of complaint — just as they were often in good heart. In their reactions to events and situations, they were simple, straightforward, direct — and predictable. When things went well, they were content, and full of quiet respect for Moses. When things went badly, they were in despair, and directed their anger at their leader.

It was understandable. After all, they were not a picked group of highly educated and devoted idealists, prepared to suffer all hard-

In the evening quails came up and covered the camp

(Exodus 16:13)

The Lord sent them quails. Migrating quails still flock to Sinai, and until recently were caught in nets. Trapping was easy, for the birds were tired after their long flight across the Mediterranean. Israel's Nature Reserve Authority has prohibited this practice.

ship to achieve their goal. They were a simple people, born bondsmen, who had been brought up without hope. They had suddenly been jerked out of their harsh but familiar life style and thrust into a strange unexpected and dangerous existence in the desert. They were virtual nomads, but without the preparation and training for nomadic life. Moses had come to them with his dream-like offer of freedom, accompanied by wondrous signs from God. To them it was thought of as a gift, presented on a miraculous tray. Although Moses must surely have told them of the trials ahead, their thinking and their power of imagination had been limited by the narrow world of their day-to-day experience. Thus, freedom to them meant above all relief from slave labor and daily beatings. True, they had gained this; and they were now beyond the reach of their Egyptian slave drivers. But was the wilderness any better, with its heat and cold, hunger and thirst, and the constant fear of attack? Moses and their tribal leaders had told them that it was: that as bondsmen they had been without a land and without a future, whereas now they were on their way

104

to both. But such talk did not fill an empty belly nor wet a parched throat.

It took time for them to realize that what Moses had offered them was not a neatly tied package labeled "freedom", but the opportunity to struggle for it. It would be one of the longest and most painful tasks of Moses' leadership — but ultimately the most rewarding — to educate his people willingly to fight and suffer for a noble ideal. When the time came for them to conquer and settle in their Promised Land, they, or rather their children, would be ready.

A GLORIOUS SURPRISE

But now, at Marah, they were complaining of thirst, and the water was brackish. God told Moses to throw a certain tree into the water which made it drinkable. After satisfying their thirst, they pressed on to Elim, where "there were twelve springs of water and seventy palm trees" (Exodus 15:27), and there the tribes encamped.

It is suggested that biblical Elim is today's oasis of Wadi Firan. Wadi means dry riverbed, and the mouth of this wadi is just off the east bank of the Gulf of Suez, about twenty miles south of Abu Rudeis. The wadi winds eastwards into Sinai, climbing between tall granite mountains until it reaches a magnificent oasis. This lies some 2,000 feet above sea level and is set amidst lofty peaks. Lush and picturesque, well watered and thick with palm trees and tamarisks, it is one of the glorious surprises of arid southern Sinai. Even the modern traveler comes upon it with joyous relief after a hot and dusty drive. To the ancient Israelites, it must have been a sight of miraculous wonder.

The next move was into the "wilderness of Sin" and they soon ran out of food. Again there was grumbling, the people angry with Moses and Aaron for taking them away from "the fleshpots" of Egypt where they "ate bread to the full" (Exodus 16:3). Moses rebuked them for complaining and then told them of the Lord's promise that he would provide "in the evening flesh to eat and in the morning bread to the full". What followed were the quails and the manna. Incidentally, these are still part of the Sinai desert life. Migrating flights of quails (small birds) come

Now the house of Israel called its name manna *(Exodus 16:31)*

This Sinai plant (*Hamada salicornica,* of the beet family) gives forth a resin-like substance which, according to some botanists, may have been the "manna" of the Bible.

they could not drink the water of Marah because it was bitter; therefore it was named Marah (Exodus 15:23)

Occasionally, as at Marah, hope turned to bitter disappointment when the thirsty Israelites came upon water and found it was brackish. Bedouin today use such water as a source of salt.

in at certain seasons to rest at night amidst the desert scrub. Up to some years ago, the Bedouin used to catch them in nets in huge quantities, for the birds would be tired after their long flight. (Since Sinai came under the administration of Israel after the 1967 Six Day War, this has been prohibited by law.) As for manna, it is described in the Bible as "a fine, flakelike thing, fine as hoar frost... like coriander seed, white, and the taste of it was like wafers made with honey" (Exodus 16:14, 31). Botanists say it calls to mind the sweetish substance that oozes out of a Sinai plant of the beet family.

Pushing deeper into the wilderness by gentle stages, they came to Rephidim and again ran out of water. This time their complaints so exasperated Moses that he cried to the Lord: "What shall I do with this people? They are almost ready to stone me" (Exodus 17:4). Moses was told to gather the elders together and in their presence strike a rock. He did so, and fresh water gushed out. (In the mountainous region of southern Sinai, there is a porous rock which gives forth water when struck.)

It was at Rephidim that the untrained Israelites, with no army organization, experienced their first battle. They were attacked by a large band of Amalekites, wild desert raiders, who must have thought the slow-moving Israelites very tempting victims. The tactic they used was to sneak up on the Israelites when these were "faint and weary" and to strike at their rear, taking them by surprise and causing casualties among "all who lagged behind". Moses immediately called on Joshua the son of Nun, of the tribe of Ephraim, and ordered him to choose a group of strong men and lead them in a counter-attack. Joshua went into action early next morning, and the ding dong battle went on through the day. Moses, accompanied by Aaron and Hur, climbed to the top of a hill which overlooked the battle-ground and gave directions by movement of "the rod of God in my hand". The Bible puts it: "Whenever Moses held up his hand, Israel prevailed; and whenever he lowered his hand, Amalek prevailed." Since his arms grew weary, Aaron and Hur held them up, and by sundown the Amalekites were defeated.

The record of this action is given in Exodus 17:8–14 (with a valuable clue to Amalekite tactics in Deuteronomy 25:18), and it contains the first mention of Joshua. He had no doubt caught the eye of Moses, possibly on one of the leader's visits of inspection to the tribes. Joshua was probably one of the clan or tribal guides whose duty it would have been to get a group of families ready for departure and shepherd them on the march. He must have impressed Moses as a bright young man with an air of authority, and he had been sent for in this moment of crisis. After his first success in combat, he became Moses' trusted personal aide — and ultimately his successor.

WISDOM FROM A DESERT CHIEF

From Rephidim the Israelites pressed deeper into the peninsula and encamped near Mount Horeb (Mount Sinai). This was the place where Moses had heard the voice from the burning bush when he had been tending his father-in-law's flocks. Jethro now heard that Moses was there and he paid him a visit. It was during this visit that Moses decided to change the way in which his people were

governed and create a more efficient system of administration.

The Bible says he took this step after receiving valuable advice from Jethro. But it is also most likely that he was influenced by the Amalekite attack — which might have ended in disaster. That attack made Moses realize that the system of authority had proved too weak, slow and complicated when challenged by a critical situation which required quick and fast action. Though he was the undisputed leader of the people, he still had to operate through the tribal and clan chiefs, and these still enjoyed a good deal of independence. Since the positions they held were handed down from father to son, they were not necessarily the most able men in their groups. And since they were concerned mostly with the interests of their particular clan or tribe, they might not always cooperate for the common good. Moses saw that this form of administration could no longer serve a people who were on their way to developing as a nation, who were now journeying through a treacherous desert, and who were threatened, as the Amalekite attack had shown, by

The rising sun, taken from the summit of Mount Sinai. The Israelites were about to receive the Ten Commandments.

surprise raids. Later, there would be more serious threats by powerful enemy armies, and they had to be prepared to meet them. The old patriarchal system had to be replaced by something like a military organization. Final authority would rest with Moses, as a kind of commander in chief; but instead of doing everything himself, he would transfer some of his duties to subordinate officers. The seniors would be responsible for large units, the junior officers for small units; but unlike army officers, they would concern themselves not only with military affairs but also, and mainly, with civil matters.

The biblical account of the formation of this new administrative framework for the nation is told as part of the charming, and seemingly simple, story of Jethro's visit to his son-in-law. The two men greeted each other warmly and spent the night catching up on each other's experiences since they last met. Moses probably told Jethro of all the wondrous things that had happened to him, and no doubt added something on the headaches and heartaches of leadership. In the morning, the shrewd old desert chief sat, watched and

110

listened while Moses gave judgement in the disputes brought before him. He saw the people milling around from morn to evening, awaiting their turn, and he heard how trivial were some of the complaints they brought. When the last case was over, Jethro said to Moses: "What you are doing is not good. You and the people with you will wear yourselves out, for the thing is too heavy for you; you are not able to perform it alone. Listen now to my voice; I will give you counsel". And he urged Moses to delegate authority. This passage in the Bible could well serve as guiding principles for every modern Faculty of Public Administration and any School of Business Administration!

Jethro told Moses that he should "choose able men from all the people, such as fear God, men who are trustworthy and who hate a bribe; and place such men over the people as rulers of thousands, of hundreds, of fifties, of tens. And let them judge the people at all times; every great matter they shall bring to you, but any small matter they shall decide themselves; so it will be easier for you, and they will bear the burden with you" (Exodus 18:17–22). Moses followed this advice, and took steps to choose his senior and junior subordinates, from "rulers of thousands" down to commanders "of tens", who would exercise administrative authority under him.

This new apparatus of government freed Moses of routine duties, and he could now apply himself, under divine guidance, to his supreme tasks: molding Hebrew society, framing their religious system and devising a code of ethics to regulate their behavior.

The high point of the freedom march through the wilderness was about to be reached — the handing down of the Law on the summit of Mount Sinai. This unique event was to shape the spiritual and physical lives of the Jewish people, stamp them with a special identity, and preserve them throughout all their monumental sufferings and disasters in the centuries that followed. It was also to have a towering influence on half the human race as the key foundation of western civilization.

CHAPTER 8 THE DRAMA ON THE MOUNT

In which a breath-taking event occurs on a mountain summit, a revolutionary treaty is forged and a unique charter for mankind issued.

The setting in which the Ten Commandments were given forth was most dramatic. (It is fully described in Chapters 19 and 20 of Exodus.) Three days before the great event, while the Israelites were encamped near the foot of Mount Sinai, Moses was called up to the mountain by the Lord. He was told to tell the people: "...if you will obey my voice and keep my covenant... you shall be to me... a holy nation". The conditions of the solemn agreement, or Covenant as it was called, were to be the Commandments, and Moses was further instructed to ask the people whether they accepted them. Moses came down the mountainside and repeated God's words to the assembled Israelites. "And all the people answered together and said, 'All that the Lord has spoken we will do'."

Moses returned to report that the people accepted the Covenant and its conditions. The Lord then ordered that the Israelites should spend the next two days purifying themselves. Thereafter he would come "in a thick cloud" to the mountain top and proclaim to Moses the text of the Covenant so "that the people may hear when I speak with you."

Dawn broke on the third day to "thunders and lightnings", and "Mount Sinai was wrapped in smoke... and the whole mountain quaked greatly". Amidst this stirring sound and sight, "God spoke all these words, saying, 'I am the Lord your God, who brought you out of the land of Egypt, out of the house of bondage. You shall have no other gods...
'You shall not make for yourself a graven image, or any likeness of anything... you shall not bow down to them...
'You shall not take the name of the Lord your God in vain...
'Remember the sabbath day, to keep it holy...
'Honor your father and your mother...
'You shall not kill.
'You shall not commit adultery.
'You shall not steal.
'You shall not bear false witness...
'You shall not covet your neighbor's house... or anything that is your neighbor's.'"

(This is the text of the Ten Commandments as they appear in Exodus 20:1–17. They are repeated with certain differences in Deuteronomy 5:6–21.)

114

ᵸᵆᵆᵆᵆᵆᵆᵆᵆᵆᵆᵆᵆᵆᵆᵆᵆᵆᵆ ᵆᵆᵆᵆᵆᵆᵆᵆ ᵆᵆᵆᵆᵆᵆ ᵆᵆᵆ
ᵆᵆᵆᵆᵆᵆ ᵆᵆᵆᵆᵆᵆᵆ ᵆᵆᵆᵆ ᵆᵆᵆᵆ
ᵆᵆᵆᵆᵆᵆ ᵆᵆᵆ ᵆᵆᵆ

Moses receiving the Law on Mount Sinai. From a 13th century illuminated Armenian translation of the Bible, in the Library of St. Thoros, Jerusalem.

THE LAWS

Those of us who live in civilized countries find nothing odd or strange or startling in these Commandments. We take for granted that it is wrong to murder, wrong to steal, wrong to worship idols, wrong to be jealous, wrong to tell lies. Even the non-religious regard the Sabbath as a vital safeguard of the health and strength of working people. We think it honorable to respect our parents. These are the normal guidelines for our behavior, and we accept them without thought, without question, almost instinctively. What most of us do not realize is that we do so precisely because of the Commandments given to the Hebrews in Sinai three thousand three hundred years ago. At that time, however, they *were* startling and revolutionary! They marked a tremendous break from the ideas, customs and behavior of the peoples of the ancient Middle East among whom the Israelites lived. They represented a giant leap forward in the whole of man's thinking in his relationship to his fellow man and to God. They signified so mighty an advance in the standards of human conduct that they remain to this day the foundations of civilized life.

In the 13th century BC, they were unique. To a pagan world which believed in many gods, the idea of monotheism, faith in the one God, was quite extraordinary. The pagans believed in the sun or the moon, a particular river or a special mountain. The God of the Hebrews was the controlling power behind all the cosmic forces, and he was everywhere, confined to no special place. The pagans worshipped "graven images" which they themselves made, in the form of men, women, birds or animals. They carved these idols in wood or shaped them in stone or pottery, put them in temples and bowed down before them, believing somehow that they became invested with the presence of deities. Sometimes their ceremonies or worship included wild dancing and drunken revelry, and sometimes the crazed slashing of their bodies until the blood flowed. It was in such a world that Moses and the Israelites proclaimed the idea of God as a spirit, invisible and without form. To do so showed tremendous insight and spiritual courage. And to ban idol worship showed equally great physical courage.

117

According to an early Christian tradition, this church near Jebel Mussa marks the spot where the Israelites made the golden calf while Moses was away on the holy mountain.

Those Commandments dealing with moral conduct created a new framework for relations between people. They stressed the supreme value of human life and the high importance of mutual respect. These principles provided the basis for preserving society and making possible its continued development. For if people were allowed to murder at will, grab whatever they fancied no matter to whom it belonged, turn their backs on family responsibilities, the result would be chaos and anarchy. Only with an orderly regulated society can there be human progress. The Ten Commandments, indeed, represented a new dimension in thought. And Moses, who received and passed them on at Mount Sinai, would have been worthy for this alone of his title as first and greatest of the Hebrew prophets and the founder of Israel.

THE CONTRACT

The Bible presents the event on Mount Sinai as a Covenant-making ceremony. It was a treaty, or agreement, or contract between God and the Children of Israel; and it could be summed up as follows: if they, the Israelites, would obey God's voice and accept his Commandments, then God would make them "a holy nation".

It is perhaps understandable that most people today, when they think of what happened at Sinai, think only of the Ten Commandments. But the Covenant itself was of the highest importance: it bound the Jewish people in a firm and permanent relationship with God. Throughout the centuries that followed, whenever the Israelites strayed from the path, turning their backs on some of the Commandments, they would be reminded by their prophets that they were breaking the Covenant — with all the serious results that that would bring—and warned to respect its conditions. This helps to explain not only the unique identity of the Jewish people but also their survival despite all the disasters they suffered.

There is a curious difference between the way in which the Israelites and the way in which the pagan peoples reacted to defeat. The reason for this difference is to be found in the Covenant. When a pagan community was conquered, it was quite ready to exchange the worship of its own idol for the idol of the victor, for his god was clearly more powerful than its own. The defeated people soon followed this up by accepting the customs and practices of the conquering enemy. After a time, they merged with the stronger nation, lost their identity and disappeared from the stage of history. The Israelites, on the other hand, when they lost a war, or were overrun, or flung into exile, did not at all think this showed that the enemy's god was more powerful than their God. Quite the reverse. They felt even more strongly that it was God who was all-powerful, and they had suffered defeat because they had broken their Covenant with him. What they had to do, therefore, was to return to the path of righteousness and observe the Commandments. Thus we find them, after every misfortune, clinging more securely to their own faith and their own customs and determined to be true to their Covenant tradition. This often involved them in grave hardship; but they stood firm, even in exile, preserved their identity — and outlived their enemies.

במדבר

ביום השביעי נשיא לבני אפרים אלישמע
בן עמיהוד קרבנו קערת כסף אחת שלשים ומאה
משקלה מזרק אחד כסף שבעים שקל בשקל
הקדש שניהם מלאים סלת בלולה בשמן למנחה
כף אחת עשרה זהב מלאה קטרת פר אחד בן בקר
איל אחד כבש אחד בן שנתו לעלה שעיר
עזים אחד לחטאת ולזבח השלמים בקר שנים
אלם חמשה עתדים חמשה כבשים בני שנה חמשה
זה קרבן אלישמע בן עמיהוד

ביום השמיני נשיא לבני מנשה גמליאל בן פדהצור
קרבנו קערת כסף אחת שלשים ומאה משקלה
מזרק אחד כסף שבעים שקל בשקל הקדש
שניהם מלאים סלת בלולה בשמן למנחה כף אחת
עשרה זהב מלאה קטרת פר אחד בן בקר איל אחד
כבש אחד בן שנתו לעלה שעיר עזים אחד לחטאת
ולזבח השלמים בקר שנים אלם חמשה עתדים
חמשה כבשים בני שנה חמשה זה קרבן גמליאל
בן פדהצור

ביום התשיעי נשיא לבני בנימן אבידן בן גדעני
קרבנו קערת כסף אחת שלשים ומאה משקלה מזרק
אחד כסף שבעים שקל בשקל הקדש שניהם
מלאים סלת בלולה בשמן למנחה כף אחת
עשרה זהב מלאה קטרת פר אחד בן בקר איל
אחד כבש אחד בן שנתו לעלה שעיר עזים אחד
לחטאת ולזבח השלמים בקר שנים אלם
חמשה עתדים חמשה כבשים בני שנה חמשה

ביום העשירי נשיא לבני דן אחיעזר בן עמישדי
קרבנו קערת כסף אחת שלשים ומאה משקלה
מזרק אחד כסף שבעים שקל בשקל הקדש שניהם
מלאים סלת בלולה בשמן למנחה כף אחת עשרה
זהב מלאה קטרת פר אחד בן בקר איל אחד עשרה
... בן שנתו לעלה שעיר עזים אחד לחטאת
ולזבח השלמים בקר שנים אלם חמשה
עתדים חמשה כבשים בני שנה חמשה זה קרבן
אחיעזר בן עמישדי

Fragments of a Torah scroll several hundred years old in the possession of a Jewish family in Peki'in, in Galilee. During the war with the Romans in the 1st century AD, this Jewish village seems to have escaped the notice of the enemy, and its inhabitants survived — and remained — when most of their compatriots were either killed or exiled. Peki'in has a record of uninterrupted Jewish settlement throughout the entire period of the Jewish dispersion.

THE PARTNERSHIP WITH GOD

We know from studies of ancient documents that the Covenant form as described in the Bible followed the normal style of treaties or agreements in the Near and Middle East during the time of Moses. But there was this big difference: whereas the normal treaty was between mortals — between individuals or groups of people — the Israelites were the first — indeed the only ones — to make a Covenant with God.

Among the more interesting covenant texts which have come down to us are the Hittite treaties of the 14th and 13th centuries BC between an emperor and a vassal. Through conquest, or the threat of attack, the powerful Hittite empire would find itself in control of territory which consisted of a number of petty kingdoms. Each would be governed by a local "king", and these "kings" would become vassals, subject to, answerable to, and dependent on the Hittite emperor. To make sure that they would not betray him, the emperor would prepare a written treaty with them. He would allow them to keep their lands and continue to rule their little

121

And he [Aaron] received the gold at their hand… and made a molten calf *(Exodus 32:4)*

The golden calf (left) was made from the melted down rings and bangles which the women brought to Aaron. Desert women (below) to this day adorn themselves with rings, bracelets and pendants.

Moses' anger burned hot, and he threw the tables out of his hands and broke them... (Exodus 32:19)

kingdoms in return for a tax and the promise of loyalty. The treaty usually stated that if the vassal kept his promise, the emperor would protect him — usually from attack by a rival empire. If he broke his promise, he would bring down upon his head the emperor's anger.

The "emperor" in the Sinai Covenant was God. The Israelites were the first to adopt the idea of the kingship of God, and they did so long before they established the mortal institution of kingship.

Thus, though the partnership with God made the Covenant unique, and its content, the Ten Commandments, made it equally unique, the covenant *form* was in common use in the region. And it was for that very reason — because it was familiar to the Israelites — that it was used. They knew, in accepting the Covenant at Sinai, that they were making a firm promise, committing themselves to a solemn treaty, taking upon themselves duties and obligations.

In the same way as the relationship between an imperial power and a vassal kingdom would be set down in a written treaty, so Israel's relationship with God had to be based on a written document. The Tablets of the Law or the Tablets of the Covenant were to be the written documents.

And now, if we go back to the Bible, we see it describes the customary covenant procedure. Moses puts the Lord's proposal to the people. Do they accept a Covenant with God? Yes, they answer. Then come its terms — the Commandments. They hear and they accept. The Covenant will then be put into writing. With that it becomes binding, and a people with a specific identity is born.

Through the Covenant and its Commandments, the Hebrew tribes, only recently freed from slavery in Egypt, became formally bound into a religious and political community.

This was also essential to promote unity; and unity was vital if Moses was to attain his major goal. His immediate aim had been to liberate them from bondage; but his ultimate purpose was to build them into a nation. To achieve this they had to be united. A common allegiance to Covenant and Commandments, binding on every member of the nation-in-the-making, was the basis for unity.

This is the law which Moses set before the children of Israe
which Moses spoke to the children of Israel when they ca

ese are the testimonies, the statutes, and the ordinances,
it of Egypt... (Deuteronomy 4:44, 45)

This is one of the earliest Hebrew copies of the Ten Commandments. It was discovered among the Dead Sea scrolls, and its date is therefore not later than the 1st century AD, though it may be even earlier.

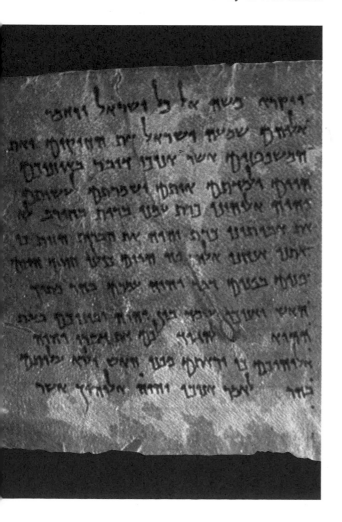

THE COVENANT CODE

The Ten Commandments set out what could be called the general principles of community policy. One scholar called them "the definition of right and wrong". But they contained no orders as to how they were to be preserved and enforced so as to ensure that the community would live up to them. This was done through a series of detailed regulations known as the Covenant Code, which put teeth into the Commandments and added flesh to their bare bones. The Code applied the aims of the Commandments to the many situations likely to arise in human society. It also decreed the punishment for those which were prohibited by the Commandments. The Covenant Code is recorded in Chapters 21 to 23 of Exodus, and follows directly after the presentation of the Ten Commandments.

The Code's regulations — called ordinances — deal with several classes of subjects. Some are religious. One, for example, instructs the community to keep three Pilgrim Festivals, Pesah (Passover), Shavuot (Feast of Weeks) and Succoth (Tabernacles), and explains when

When Moses came down from Mount Sinai ... the skin of his face shone because he had been talking with God

(Exodus 34:29)

The Moses of Michelangelo, a work of genius by the 16th century master, in the Church of S. Pietro in Vincoli, in Rome. Moses is shown with horns in his head because of a mistranslation in the Latin Bible read by the artist. The Hebrew word for "horn" is similar to, and was mistaken for, the Hebrew word for "shone", which the Bible uses to describe Moses' glowing countenance as he came down from Mount Sinai.

and how to observe them. Another one orders that the "first fruits" of one's produce should be given up to "the house of the Lord". Yet another prescribes capital punishment for pagan worship.

Many of the ordinances, however, deal with secular, or non-sacred affairs, like crime, such as murder or theft; the treatment of slaves; and compensation for damage to persons and property.

The most interesting, perhaps, are those which might be called moral guidelines. There are ordinances which warn people not "to pervert justice", not to "utter a false report", not to "join hands with a wicked man". "You shall take no bribe," says another. Some showed an unusual humaneness for those times: "You shall not wrong a stranger or oppress him, for you were strangers in the land of Egypt". And: "If you lend money to any of my people with you who is poor... you shall not exact interest from him". And there is this one, which shows such kindness and understanding: "If ever you take your neighbor's garment in pledge [for security, or in payment of a debt], you shall

restore it to him before the sun goes down; for that is his only covering, it is his mantle for his body; in what else shall he sleep?"

There was nothing like this in any of the other ancient codes, not even in the sophisticated ones like the Hittite Code of the 14th century BC, or the more noted 18th century BC Code of Hammurabi, the king of Babylonia. These codes were issued in the name of the mortal king. In the Covenant Code, the "author" was God. The difference was basic, for it affected the very nature of law and justice. Under the Covenant Code, the law was divine, and so crimes were sins, a violation of God's will. In the other codes, the law, man-made, could be based on what the king thought expedient or advantageous; it was not necessarily based on principle. Thus, in the Hammurabi Code, for example, the penalties for offences varied according to the social status of the offenders. In the Covenant Code, the law was supreme, and all persons, high and low, were equal before the law. In the Covenant Code, the measure of punishment had to fit the measure of the sin against the Lord. In the other codes, the punishment

Idols from early historical periods grouped for display in Jerusalem's Rockefeller Museum. The idea of monotheism in the First Commandment and the ban on idol-worship in the Second were revolutionary and courageous in the pagan world of Israelite times.

often depended on the political, economic or social circumstances of the community. Thus, certain types of theft carried the death penalty. Under the Covenant Code, no offence against property was ever punishable by death.

Israelite law was imbued by the highest religious and moral values; in the other ancient codes, the guiding values were largely political and economic.

The 18th century BC "stele of Hammurabi", an 8-foot high stone monument. The upper part shows the great Babylonian king standing before the god Marduk. The writing below, in the Akkadian language, are some of the clauses in the Code of Hammurabi.

CHAPTER 9 THE BROKEN STONES

*In which an extraordinary deed of treachery
is committed during Moses' absence, and
the culprits are given a novel punishment.*

When the first stage of the Sinai ceremonies was over, Moses was again called to the summit of the mount to receive the written document of the Covenant — "the tables [tablets] of stone, with the law and the commandment, which I have written for their [the people's] instruction" (Exodus 24:12). (It must be remembered that in those early days, one did not write on parchment or paper. That came only centuries later. At the time of Moses, one wrote by carving out letters on pottery or — when the document was very important — on stone.)

Moses left Aaron and Hur in charge of the encampment, and went up the mountainside "with his servant Joshua". About half-way up, he told Joshua to wait, and he himself continued alone, disappearing into the cloud which covered the top of Sinai. There he stayed forty days and forty nights communing with the Lord. While he was away, the people below persuaded Aaron to "make us gods", and Aaron made them a "molten calf" (Exodus 32:4) which they worshipped with sacrifices, feastings and pagan dancing.

What could have led them to take such an extraordinary step — and so soon after the initial Covenant ceremony? It seems absolutely shocking that having heard and solemnly accepted the terms of the Covenant, and while it was being put down in writing, they should suddenly break the very foundations upon which the Covenant rested.

The Bible gives no explanation, simply stating the facts of what happened. But the way in which they are stated offers us three clues to the thinking of the Israelites which may explain how they came to take the action they did. The Bible says that the people approached Aaron when they "saw that Moses delayed to come down from the mountain", and they said: "as for this Moses...we do not know what has become of him" (Exodus 32:1). The clues lie in "Moses delayed"; in their not knowing "what has become of him"; and above all in the contemptuous words "as for this Moses".

We can now imagine the scene among the people in the encampment near the foot of the mountain while Moses is away. He has not told them that he will be gone for almost six weeks. All they know is that he has dis-

Moses erected the tabernacle; he laid its bases, and s
and he spread the tent over the tabernacle, ...as the Lo

appeared in a cloud near the summit, and will presumably be back soon. They wait a day, two days, three days. He does not appear. By the end of a week, he still has not returned and they begin to be worried. By the end of the second week they are alarmed, and as the days pass they become convinced that he is dead. This throws them into a state of terror. For if he is dead, then all his grand promises are clearly worthless. He had come to them with brave and mighty words, spoken as the emissary of God, and they had believed him. But now he has vanished, and so he was probably not what he claimed to be; or if he was, he has obviously been abandoned by God. In that case, they, the people, are left high and dry, stranded in the harsh desert.

It was no doubt when they reached this mood that those clan leaders who had earlier objected to the limitation of their authority began to incite the people against Moses, possibly suggesting that they return to Egypt. It may have been these leaders who proposed that they make a graven image; and if any objected that this was in direct breach of the Covenant, they might have replied that it had

Aaron the High Priest consecrates the Tabernacle, as imagined by the artist who did this wall painting in the 3rd century synagogue of Dura-Europos.

134

its frames, and put in its poles, and raised up its pillars;
d commanded Moses *(Exodus 40:18, 19)*

not yet been put into writing and its laws, therefore, were not yet in force.

TREACHERY

It must be remembered that only about one year had passed since they had left Egypt. They had not yet shaken off their slave mentality. They were still far from being a united nation with a strong collective will. They were still a loose group of clans who had followed the call of a great personality and magnetic leader, Moses. But now he was apparently dead, and there had not been time for him to train others who could take over the leadership, nor time enough to put through the administrative reforms suggested by Jethro. Without Moses, the people felt helpless, forsaken, far from the homes they had left and with no compass for the future. They therefore agreed to the suggestion of the inciters to resort to the devices they had witnessed in Egypt when their neighbors had sought help in time of deep trouble.

(Some scholars say that the golden calf may have been shaped like Apis, the sacred bull of Egypt, which they would have seen being worshipped by the Egyptians. Others say that they were really worshipping God — as witness Aaron's proclamation that there "shall be a feast to the Lord" — and that only outwardly did the worship appear Egyptian.)

The Bible says that God had told Moses what was happening below and had threatened to destroy the people, but Moses pleaded for them and God relented. However, when Moses eventually came down from the mountain and saw for himself what was going on, he took "the two tables of the testimony... tables that were written on both sides...and broke them at the foot of the mountain." He was of course shocked, bitter, furious. His "anger burned hot", and his action is understandable as having been taken in a fit of rage. But there may be an additional reason why he broke the tablets. What his people were doing was a direct breach of the first and second of the Ten Commandments. They were breaking the terms of the Covenant. The Covenant was therefore no longer in force. It was the custom in the region that when this happened, and treaties were no longer valid, the treaty document was destroyed. This, then, is what

Moses, the mediator of the Covenant, did. By breaking the tablets of stone, he was destroying the written document of the Covenant. If the relationship between the Israelites and God was to be renewed, the Covenant document would have to be written on new tablets.

Moses was still in a state of fierce anger when he reached the encampment, determined on firm action to re-establish control and pull the people together. He promptly burnt the golden calf, had it ground into powder, mixed it with water and forced the people to swallow it. He then called upon his own tribe of Levites to put to death many of the pagan worshippers.

His action was timely and effective. The people were repentant. And his authority was now greater than ever. His very reappearance had given heart to the faithful, shamed the doubters who thought him dead, and confounded those — probably the inciting clan leaders — who had spoken jeeringly of "this Moses" and led the others astray. More important, here was a new side to Moses' character which they had not seen before,

nor suspected. They knew him as a leader who had never used force; who had led them by example, and with words of encouragement alone. He now showed that when necessary he could be hard and ruthless. The people would not easily forget his swift judgement and action.

If until now they had respected his persuasive tone, they would now also fear his iron hand. Not all, though most of them. Some of the discontented would continue their opposition. It would be soft-pedaled for the time being; but it would grow sharper as the effects of what had just happened would begin to wear off. It would eventually erupt into open conflict. But for the moment, the people were subdued. Moses could now mediate the renewal of the Covenant, and receive a newly written document. He could again make the ascent to the sacred mountain, and again stay there forty nights and forty days, confident that his people would not repeat their breach of moral discipline.

A CURIOUS ERROR

He went up carrying two stone tablets which

a very loud trumpet [shofar] blast, so that all the people who were in the camp trembled (Exodus 19:16)

Simchat Torah, Hebrew for "Rejoicing of the Law", is the last day of the Pilgrim Festival of Succoth, when Jews in olden times went up to the Temple in Jerusalem to express their joy in the Torah. Since the re-unification of Jerusalem during the 1967 Six Day War, Jews can once again celebrate the Festival close to the site of the Temple, at the Western Wall (left). The sound of the shofar (below), the traditional ram's horn used in Jewish ritual, is again heard here.

had been freshly hewed to replace the ones he had broken. When he came down, with "the words of the covenant, the ten commandments", newly engraved on the stones, Aaron and the Israelites saw that "the skin of his face shone", radiating such light that "they were afraid to come near him" (Exodus 34:30). But he called them all to a solemn assembly, and read out to them what had been written in the Covenant.

(This description in the Bible of the glowing expression on Moses' face as he came down the mountain inspired one of the greatest works of art by one of the greatest artists who ever lived. This was the celebrated sculpture of Moses by Michelangelo [1475–1564], now in the Church of S. Pietro in Vincoli, in Rome. However, it has a rather curious feature: Moses is represented with horns in his head, and visitors often wonder why. They would be surprised to learn that this is due to a wrong translation of the original Hebrew of the Bible referring to "the skin of his [Moses'] face", which "shone".

This is how the error came about. The Hebrew for "shone" is "karan". But since

139

Hebrew is written without vowels, "karan" appears in writing simply as three consonants, "k r n". The trouble is that there is another Hebrew word, "keren", which is also written with the same consonants "k r n". This is confusing to people who do not know Hebrew; but those who do, know from the sense of the phrase which word is intended. However, there is a further complication, for "keren" has two meanings. One is "ray", the other is "horn". The translation of the Bible available to Michelangelo was the Latin [Vulgate] translation used during the Middle Ages, and in it the verb "karan" was mistaken for the noun "keren" and mistranslated as "horn". Thus, the strange feature of Michelangelo's masterpiece is the product of a double literary lapse — the wrong reading of the Hebrew word, and even that wrongly translated!)

During his first stay on Mount Sinai, Moses had received from the Lord detailed instructions for building an Ark of acacia wood covered with gold in which the Tablets of the Law would be kept. Aaron and his sons were to be ordained as priests to take care of it. Moses now set the craftsmen among his people to build this Ark of the Covenant, or Ark of the Law, as it was called. The Ark would accompany the Children of Israel throughout their journeyings.

CHAPTER 10 THE SPIES

*In which intelligence agents report on
their mission – with surprising results.*

It was now thirteen months since the Israelites had left Egypt, and they were about to move on from the area of Mount Sinai towards the Promised Land.

Moses took two important steps before they set out. He ordered a military census — taking a detailed count of the men in all the tribes who were fit for battle; and he commanded that from now on there would be a fixed order of march.

The census covered all able-bodied men from the age of twenty and upwards. It was carried out tribe by tribe by Moses and Aaron. In each tribe they were accompanied by the tribal leader. Only one tribe was left out of this census (though it was counted separately, later, and included "every male from a month old and upward"). This was the tribe of Levi. The Levites would provide no soldiers, for they would have charge of the Ark and all that went with it, at all times, in peace and war, carrying it when they were on the move and setting it up when they halted. The Bible gives the results of the census. The total number of men "able to go forth to war" (Numbers 1:46) was 603,550. (Most modern scholars think the number must have been much smaller.)

To ensure that they would cross the desert in a disciplined manner — or with as much discipline and good order as it was possible to expect from a group not of trained soldiers but of civilians, men and women, old and young — Moses gave each tribe a fixed position both in the order of march and when they halted and pitched camp. The people were organized into four sub-groups, each of three tribes. When they came to a resting place, instead of flopping down wherever they happened to be, they would range themselves into a square. Each side of the square would consist of one sub-group, each with a distinctive standard. At every halt they would take up the same positions: the tribe of Judah would head one sub-group, together with Issachar and Zebulun, and would encamp on the east; Reuben, with Simeon and Gad on the south; Ephraim, Manasseh and Benjamin on the west; and Dan, Asher and Naphtali on the north. All would thus be facing the open square. In the center would stand the Tabernacle. This was a mobile structure,

the name of that place was called Kibroth-hatta'avah,
because there they buried the people who had the craving

(Numbers 11:34)

Ancient tombs recently discovered in southern Sinai. They are associated locally with Kibroth Hatta'avah (graves of the craving) of Numbers 11:34, where many Israelites died after gorging themselves with meat.

shaped like a tent, which could be taken to pieces and re-assembled. It housed the Ark of the Covenant. Surrounding the Tabernacle, also inside the square, would be the tents of the Levites.

When they got the signal to move, they would do so in the following order. Judah's sub-group would lead off, followed by some Levites with the Tabernacle, which they had dismantled. Then Reuben's contingent, followed by other Levites carrying the Ark and the interior furnishings of the Tabernacle. After them would come Ephraim's sub-group; and Dan's contingent would bring up the rear. Within each tribe, the clans were also given fixed positions. The signal to move and to halt would be given by trumpet calls. The trumpet would also be used to sound a general alarm.

INTELLIGENCE MISSION

The tribes now set off, following their new disciplined march pattern, and for the next few months they trekked slowly through the desert. This part of the journey was fairly quiet and peaceful. They met no raiders, no hostile bands, no enemy forces; or, if they did, there is no record of it. It is likely that since they were now better organized to beat off the kind of assault which they had suffered earlier by the Amelekite raiders, any marauding brigands on the hunt for loot would think twice before molesting them. However, this did not mean that Moses could now relax. It is true that he was not as overworked as he was before. He had put into force his administrative reform plan and appointed trusted assistants who could take over from him many of his lesser day-to-day duties. But he still carried the burden of overall responsibility, and he was given much cause for worry. As the Israelites trudged on week by week across the endless wastes of sand, many of them became irritable, quarrelsome and bad-tempered, grumbling about the heat, the cold, sickness, hunger and thirst. It was Moses who had to deal with their discontent.

He did so with firmness, but with sympathy and understanding; for he recognized that, unlike himself, who had had several years' experience of desert conditions, his people were quite new to them. They were not like Bedouin whose life and future were tied to the desert and who had therefore adapted themselves to its harshness and its meager benefits and created for themselves a special way of living. For the Israelites, the wilderness was simply a stretch of parched land to be crossed as quickly as possible so that they could reach and settle down in their Promised Land. To the desert nomad, each day might be an exciting challenge. To the Israelite, it was a hardship to be suffered. And as the days extended to weeks, and the weeks to months, they grew more gloomy. When oh when would it end?

It was with a sense of supreme relief that, two years, after they left Egypt, the Israelites arrived at the rich fresh greenery of Kadesh Barnea, and Moses said they could rest. They could not know that they would be resting there for the next thirty-eight years.

Kadesh Barnea is a large oasis near the northeastern edge of the Sinai peninsula, some fifty miles south of Beersheba, close to the southern entrance to the land of Canaan.

Thus, the Israelites were now at the threshold of the Promised Land. But they knew very little about that land. They knew that it was not like Egypt, with settled boundaries and a strong central administration. They knew that Canaan was a piece of territory which lay between two rival empires, and that it had no defined frontiers and no single all-powerful ruler (like the Pharaoh of Egypt). They also knew that it was thinly populated; that some of its inhabitants were already established in cities and villages, each ruled by a local "king"; and that others continued a nomadic life, moving around with their flocks in search of pasture and dwelling in tents.

So much Moses and the Israelites knew. But before they could attempt to enter this country, they needed to know very much more. They needed information on the actual size of its mixed population, and where each group was living; whether they were hostile or friendly, tough or easy-going; what kind of weapons they possessed; and whether their cities were open or fortified with walls. They also required to know something about the topography of the country; about its fertility

— whether the soil was fruitful or barren; and about its climate and its sources of water.

There was only way to find out: send in a small group of observers who would travel around discreetly, keep their eyes and ears open, and come back to report what they had seen and heard. In order not to cause jealousy among the tribes, Moses picked a team consisting of twelve men, one from each tribe. And he tried to ensure that each man was an outstanding officer who was respected by his tribe. Joshua, for example, was the man he chose as the representative of the tribe of Ephraim.

Moses called them together and gave them detailed instructions on what he wanted them to look for particularly. In the language of modern armies, this is called "a briefing"; the task they were sent on is called "a reconnaissance mission"; and the team itself is called either "a reconnaissance team" or "an intelligence unit" — their object being to gather information. The Bible does not use these fancy terms. It uses a good old-fashioned word, saying that Moses told them "to spy out the land of Canaan"; and ever since the

As they journeyed through the wilderness, the Israelites would often come across bleak stretches like this, and they would tread the parched and cracked surface with despair in their hearts.

members of the team have been known as "the twelve spies".

In his detailed briefing, Moses instructed them to "Go up into the Negev yonder, and go up into the hill country, and see what the land is, and whether the people who dwell in it are strong or weak, whether they are few or many, and whether the land that they dwell in is good or bad, and whether the cities that they dwell in are camps or strongholds... and whether there is wood in it or not. Be of good courage, and bring some of the fruit of the land" (Numbers 13:19, 20).

THE "GIANT" AND THE "GRASSHOPPER"

The twelve observers slipped out of Kadesh, quietly entered Canaan and spent forty days on their mission, collecting information on the main areas of the country. On their return, as soon as they entered the Israelite encampment, everyone could see at least one item which would certainly appear in their report. This was a branch of a vine from which hung a single cluster of grapes. The bunch was so large and heavy that it had to be carried on a

And the people of Israel ...stayed in Kadesh

(Numbers 20:1)

It was with supreme relief that the Israelites reached the sweet waters and fresh greenery of the oasis of Kadesh Barnea. It was close to the southern edge of the Promised Land, which they hoped they would soon be entering. But they were to remain here for the next 38 years, and for most of the adults who had set out on the Exodus, this was journey's end.

pole slung between two men. It had been picked near Hebron. They also brought back juicy pomegranates and luscious figs.

These impressive fruits were an appetizing illustration of the unanimous opinion of all twelve spies, expressed in symbolic language, that the land "flows with milk and honey" (Numbers 13:27). They said this at the beginning of their report, which was presented to Moses and Aaron at a general assembly. However, they went on to say that the people in the country were "strong"; that some of them were "descendants of Anak" — "anak" is the Hebrew for "giant"; and that their cities were "fortified and very large". They gave details, noting that the hilly regions were inhabited by Hittites, Jebusites and Amorites; the Amelekites held the Negev; and the Canaanites occupied the coastal plain and the Jordan valley.

So far, their report had been factual. It was a straightforward account of what they had seen and heard on their mission. This part of the report was unanimous. But then came the second function of any intelligence report, and this was a matter of judgement: what to

148

The "people journeyed to Hazeroth" (Numbers 11:35). "Hazeroth" is Hebrew for "fences", and the name may have been descriptive of the place. Here is an unusual example of a fenced plantation in today's southern Sinai.

make of the facts, what inferences to draw from them, what action to take. On this, the twelve were divided, and by no means equally. Only two thought that the Israelites should move north without delay — they were not many miles from the southern rim of Canaan; and although the local inhabitants might be "strong", and would put up tough opposition, "we are well able to overcome" them. This view was voiced by Caleb, of the tribe of Judah, and he was tacitly supported by Joshua. But the other ten recommended the exact opposite. They said there was little hope in defeating the people they would come up against in Canaan, for they "are stronger than we" (Numbers 13:31). To dramatize their argument, the ten gave the general assembly a graphic description of just how heavy the odds against them would be if they tried to enter Canaan now. Some of the people there were of such "great stature", they said, that compared to them "we seemed ... like grasshoppers."

PANDEMONIUM

This picture of the "giant" (anak) versus the "grasshoppers" was so vivid that all who heard it were gripped by fear and panic. Within minutes, pandemonium broke out. The people rose in anger against Moses. He had misled them, deluded them. He had taken them on a lengthy march, full of suffering, through the desert; he had strung them along with rosy promises of freedom; and now all he could offer them was the point of the enemy's sword. Canaan might be a fine country; it might be the Promised Land; but they would all be killed trying to get in. They would have been better off if they had stayed in Egypt. Someone even shouted above the clamor that they should choose another leader to take them back there.

The assembly was charged with tension. The mood was inflammable. And this was just the kind of proposal to spark a mutiny. In this critical situation, up jumped Joshua and Caleb, and without repeating their earlier suggestion that they go into battle immediately, they tried to quiet the people with the assurance that God was on their side and they would defeat their enemies. They were almost stoned for their efforts.

151

Moses sent the twelve scouts into Canaan, and this is an illuminated manuscript containing the biblical account of their 40-day intelligence mission. It is the work of a Jewish artist and scribe who lived in Egypt at the beginning of the 12th century AD.

152

ויתורו. ל ויתרו ל ויתמלדו ל ויתמרו. לס:
לב: ל ל:

אֶל־מֹשֶׁה

שְׁלַח־לְךָ אֲנָשִׁים

וְיָתֻרוּ אֶת־אֶרֶץ כְּנַעַן

אֲשֶׁר אֲנִי נֹתֵן לִבְנֵי

יִשְׂרָאֵל אִישׁ אֶחָד

אִישׁ אֶחָד לְמַטֵּה

אֲבֹתָיו תִּשְׁלָחוּ כֹּל נָשִׂיא

תשלחו ב וסימנתדון למטה אבתיו
תשלחו ואגמרי לא תשלחו ס:

The Bible says that because of the people's outburst, which showed that they had no faith in the divine promises, God decided that they would remain in the desert for forty years until all the adults had died out, except for Joshua and Caleb. Only those who were now infants would be privileged to enter the Promised Land.

The Bible does not tell us how the rowdy meeting of the general assembly ended. It is likely, however, that since no quick decision was to be taken, the people eventually dispersed, angry and bitter, thinking that they would continue the discussion among themselves next day. Moses and Aaron probably retired to consult with Joshua and Caleb and review the military prospects in greater detail.

Moses must have come to the conclusion that an immediate invasion of southern Canaan, as Caleb had suggested, was not practical. True, this was the shortest and most direct route; but it would bring them into battle with the strongly fortified Amalekites and Canaanites, and for this the Israelites were not yet ready. As the meeting had shown, their morale was low, so that even if they had been skilled soldiers — which they were not — they lacked the necessary fighting spirit. It was clear that military action would have to be delayed — long enough to train a vigorous army. And that army would have to be drawn from the younger generation. (Ibn Ezra [1089–1164], the great poet, philosopher, scientist and Bible commentator, suggested that the "generation of the wilderness", who had lived most of their years as slaves, were unsuited, psychologically, for the tough battles which had to be fought to enter and settle in the Promised Land.)

Moses no doubt called the tribal elders next day and told them that the people could stop worrying. There would be no immediate move. They would remain in Kadesh Barnea for the time being, close to water and grazing grounds. Thus, they need fear no clash with the "giants" in the near future.

This must have calmed the majority. But there was one group who may have been ashamed and angered by the behavior of the general assembly, and who took it into their heads to make a quick dash to the border of

All twelve spies reported on the magnificent fruits that grew (and grow today) in the Promised Land, and they brought back specimens. Among them was the nutritious and honey-sweet fig.

Canaan and tackle the enemy. Moses may have been pleased with their show of spirit, but he told them that they would be disobeying orders. The time for action was not yet ripe. They were eager, and they persisted; so Moses warned them that they "will not succeed", for the Lord would not be "among you" and the Ark of the Covenant would not be with them. But they would not listen to his warning. They went off — and suffered a severe defeat.

After this unofficial and unsuccessful attempt to invade Canaan from the south, the Israelites settled down to live the life of nomadic herdsmen in the wilderness of Zin — northeastern Sinai and the northwestern Negev. Kadesh Barnea remained their base.

*the land... flows with milk and honey, and this is
its fruit* *(Numbers 13:27)*

The desert-worn Israelites gazed with wonder at the
luscious grapes (left). They were so heavy with juice
that a single vine branch had to be carried on a
pole slung between two men. The pomegranates
(below) were also a welcome sight, their richness
held within ripened skins of crimson and gold.

CHAPTER 11 THE GIANT STEP

*In which the leader of a people comes to an
unexpected end within sight of his goal.*

Having to stay at Kadesh Barnea when he was
so near to the Promised Land must have been
a heavy blow to Moses. There can be little
doubt that he had both hoped and planned
to enter Canaan as soon as the Exodus
journey across the wilderness was over. It was
clear to him now that this was not possible.
His planned timetable was no longer real-
istic. What led him to this sad conclusion was
the frightened and undisciplined reaction of
his people to the reported strength of the
local population in southern Canaan. The
Israelites were obviously scared by the pros-
pect of serious battle. It was equally obvious
that they were not yet ready to undertake the
heavy tasks of nationhood. More time was
needed to prepare them for their role of
destiny.

Moses had been trying to do this for the
previous two years — and he had indeed
brought them a long way, geographically and
spiritually, from the frontiers of Egypt. He
had tried to unify them, make them a disciplined group, strengthen their bodies and
spirits, raise their sights, set them high ideals
of a unique religious and moral code, imbue

them with faith in God — and in themselves.
These were great goals. But it was perhaps
unreasonable to expect them to be reached in
so short a time.

Writing a law is not enough. The public
has to be educated to understand the whys
and wherefores of the law, and to reach the
point where they accept it and respect it
almost instinctively. This cannot be done
overnight. It also takes time for a people to
get used to a new pattern of living, a new
outlook, new customs, a new system of
administration. Moses had perhaps not realized this while they were wandering through
the desert, possibly because he had managed
to achieve so much during that period. But he
realized it now. Like all great leaders — whose
very greatness lies in their being way ahead
of the public — he had been impatient. He
was always trying to force the pace, to
straighten the bowed backs of the former
slaves with a single jerk, to push them to run
free when they were barely crawling. Now, at
Kadesh Barnea, he knew that certain process-
es cannot be skipped. He had to set about
with painstaking care to build the federation

the people of Israel… came into the wilderness of Zin

(Numbers 20:1)

The wilderness of Zin was the backdrop to Kadesh Barnea. When
the time came to leave, Moses was unwilling to risk immediate
combat by taking the short route into southern Canaan. Instead,
he led his people on a lengthy detour, turning first south to the
Gulf of Eilat and then swinging northeast into Trans-Jordan.

of tribes into a hardy, close-knit community, ready and willing to meet the challenges of the future. It was to take almost another four decades.

He began the slow but essential task of educating his people. They had to learn what were the responsibilities of civilized nationhood. And Moses had to provide them with a spiritual reservoir rich enough to sustain them in their long struggle. He developed the religious code, extended the civil laws, laid down rituals of worship, and specified the duties of the priestly tribe of Levites. He guided and trained subordinates who would help him in the administration, and who would form the broad leadership in the future. He tightened discipline, and when the time was judged ripe, there was stern punishment for breaches of the Covenant Code. The biblical account of this period at Kadesh contains the first record of a man being sentenced to death by stoning for "gathering sticks on the sabbath day" (Numbers 15:32), a breach of the Fourth Commandment.

Carrying out this penalty must have come as a shock to the community. It may well have touched off the revolt which is reported in the biblical chapter which follows. The rebellion was led by Korah, Dathan and Abiram, and it was supported by two hundred and fifty elders, all "well-known men" (Numbers 16:2). Some of them were probably clan leaders who had resented the limitation of their power ever since Moses had appeared on the scene. They now rose up and directly challenged the leadership of Moses and Aaron. But Moses was now strong enough to crush them. In a dramatic example to the community, the Lord caused the earth to open and swallow up the rebel leaders, while their supporters were consumed by fire.

The only other outstanding event recorded at Kadesh was the strange lapse of Moses himself in not following the exact command of the Lord. It happened during a period of drought, and as usual the people gathered before Moses and Aaron in fierce complaint over the lack of water for themselves and their animals. The episode is similar to the one at Rephidim (mentioned in Chapter 7, page 5). But whereas on that occasion Moses had been told to strike the rock, he was now ordered by the Lord to "tell the rock... to yield its water." In an untypical action, Moses, instead of speaking to the rock, lifted his rod and struck it twice, and out gushed water in abundance. He had apparently doubted that the rock would give forth its waters if he simply spoke to it. He had obviously been impatient, concerned only with getting quick results and satisfying the clamoring crowd. But he had shown a disbelief in divine power, and this was a particularly grave sin for him, since he was the leader of the people and he had to set the supreme example of faith. The punishment was accordingly harsh. "Because you did not believe in me" (Numbers 20:12), said the Lord, Moses and Aaron would not be privileged to enter the Promised Land. (Their sister Miriam had died earlier at Kadesh and was buried there.)

The years went by. The infants who had been born and brought up in the wilderness and had never experienced slavery in Egypt were now young adults. Though it is not mentioned in the Bible, it seems likely, from what happened later, that the males among them were now given military training, probably under the direction of Joshua. They were the ones who would be doing most of the front line fighting if anyone tried to stop them when they eventually crossed into Canaan. Here at Kadesh they could learn the basic skills of warfare. It was hoped that when put to the test, they would prove battleworthy.

THE LAST LAP

The moment had come to leave Kadesh and press on towards their goal. The young generation were as ready as tough training could make them. But they were as yet untried, and Moses was unwilling to risk a major military action — and possible defeat — too soon. He therefore decided against an approach to Canaan from the south, which, as we have seen, was the quickest route, and would have brought them to the border within two or three days. He preferred a very much longer route, one which would bring them to Canaan from the east, across the river Jordan. It would take much time, several months in fact; but he would gain two

An inlet near Eilat which the Israelites passed on their journeyings, and today a favorite picnic and bathing site for their descendants.

162

advantages: his young soldiers would gain fighting experience in the probable raiding attacks and skirmishes en route; and when they did reach Canaan from an unexpected direction, the potential enemy would be taken by surprise.

The easiest way to get to the east bank of the river Jordan from Kadesh was to cross the northern Negev to a point just south of the Dead Sea, and then move northwards in trans-Jordan along the King's Highway. This was the main caravan route from the south to Damascus and Mesopotamia in the north. But this route lay through the lands of Edom and Moab. Moses was reluctant to provoke them. He therefore sent messengers to the king of Edom asking permission to pass peacefully through his territory. He undertook to stick to the "King's Highway" and promised not to take water from any of his wells — or to pay compensation if he did. The request was refused. Moses therefore decided to make an even more lengthy detour.

He turned south, and marched to Etzion Geber at the head of the Gulf of Eilat (as it is known today). He then swung round in a wide arc and came northeast, thus avoiding Edom and passing it to the east. Some scholars say that he came north, bypassed Edom from the west, and went right through Moab. The majority, however, favor the longer, more circuitous route. They hold that the Israelites, after bypassing Edom from the east, continued northwards along the eastern highlands of trans-Jordan and skirted the eastern edge of Moab until they reached the Arnon river.

The lands to the north of this river were now being ruled by a certain Sihon king of the Amorites, who had conquered it shortly before from Moab. Sihon's capital was Heshbon, which was on the east bank of the river Jordan roughly opposite Jericho. Jericho lay inside Canaan, on the west bank of the river. Thus, to get into Canaan, the Israelites had to travel through Sihon's territory. Moses therefore sent him a message asking permission to cross his land. Sihon not only refused, but backed his refusal by sending forth his army to drive the Israelites off. Unlike their earlier reaction when they had been refused by the king of Edom and had simply

164

they…encamped on the other side of the Arnon, which is.
Sihon king of the Amorites… fought against Israel. A.

The Mountains of Edom, which the Israelites
bypassed after the king of Edom had
refused them permission to cross his territory.

e boundary of Moab, between Moab and the Amorites...
rael slew him (Numbers 21:11, 13, 21, 23, 24)

The plains of Moab. The Israelites skirted
this land, then met the Amorites in a
major battle, and gained their first decisive victory.

When the ass saw the angel of the Lord, she lay down under Balaam; and Balaam's anger was kindled, and he struck the ass with his staff (Numbers 22:27)

Rembrandt's painting of Balaam and his donkey. Balaam, a fortune teller, was sent by the frightened king of Moab to curse the Israelites. He set out on his donkey, but on the way the animal stopped. Balaam beat it unmercifully, but it obstinately refused to go on, for it saw what its master, at first, could not see: an angel with drawn sword hovering over the path. Eventually, when Balaam tried to curse the Israelites, he could voice only blessings.

turned and taken another route, the Israelites this time stood their ground, and fighting followed. Though there had been some skirmishing along the way, this was their first decisive battle; and in this crucial military test, the new generation of Hebrews, better organized and better trained than their parents had been, proved their mettle. They defeated Sihon's forces, captured Heshbon, and swept away his regime. They were soon in occupation of his entire territory, from the river Arnon in the south to the river Jabbok in the north.

They pressed on even farther north into Gilead right up to the river Yarmuk. King Og of Bashan led his army in an attack against them, and was defeated. (Bashan is the area north of the Yarmuk which is known today as the Golan Heights.) The Israelites now occupied the whole belt along the eastern bank of the river Jordan. They were bounded by Moab in the south and Ammon in the east. Here they remained for a while, building up their strength, improving their military organization, and awaiting a suitable moment to cross into Canaan.

Meanwhile, news of their battle successes had spread quickly through the neighboring lands, and caused much anxiety to the local rulers. The one most afraid that he might suffer the fate of the Amorite king Sihon was Balak, the king of Moab; for, as we have seen, Sihon's territory had been conquered earlier from the Moabites, and if the Israelites could defeat Sihon, they were certainly strong enough to defeat the Moabite king. Balak therefore sent for a well-known soothsayer, Balaam, to come and curse the Israelites "since they are too mighty for me; perhaps I shall be able to defeat them and drive them from the land; for I know that he whom you bless is blessed, and he whom you curse is cursed" (Numbers 22:6). What followed was the celebrated episode of Balaam and his ass, who kept wanting to stop, and the even more celebrated switch from curses to blessings: when Balaam opened his mouth to curse Israel as Balak wished, a blessing slipped out instead: "How fair are your tents, O Jacob, your encampments, O Israel!" (Numbers 24:5).

Another census taken at this time showed that of all the men who had been in Egypt and had experienced the Exodus, only three were left alive — Joshua, Caleb and Moses himself. Aaron had died at Mount Hor, whose location is not known, soon after leaving Kadesh.

LOOKING BACK — AND FORWARD

The Hebrews would soon be taking the great step for which the Exodus from Egypt and their long freedom trek through the wilderness had been but a preparation — entry into the Promised Land. It would be charged with danger; for although much of the land was empty, they could expect stiff opposition from nomadic groups who had come in before them, and who were strongly established in key areas. Thanks to Moses, they were now ready to meet this challenge.

It was he, under divine guidance, who had rallied their parents to resistance, broken their chains of slavery and led them safely through the desert. It was he who had mediated God's Covenant with the people, framing unique religious and ethical principles which gave them — and would preserve for

Moses went up...the Lord showed him all the land...And ...said...I will give it to your descendants (Deuteronomy 34:1–4)

Moses could look down at the narrow river Jordan (below) and see the shallow fords which the Israelites would cross to reach Canaan. The view to the west took in the mountains of Ephraim (right), the central range of the future Land of Israel which he was allowed to glimpse but not enter.

all time — a specific identity. It was he who had laid the basis of a national discipline by providing a central legal system and a central form of worship. And it was through him that the tribes and clans were now a nation in the making.

Moses had done all this by kindling and keeping alive the spirit of freedom. With his eye firmly fixed on the goal of liberation, he had urged his people forward, at times gentle, at times tough, caring for them, guiding them, giving them encouragement in moments of despair, seeking at all times to fill their hearts with his own sense of purpose.

His work was now done. He had lived long. He could look back on a record of noble achievement. But he could also feel the pain of sharp disappointment. He had hoped that promise and fulfillment could be spanned in one generation, the generation who had known slavery. He had believed that they could march to his pace, be fired by his own burning urgency and his own visionary ideals. Only at Kadesh had he come to understand that the immense task of conquest and settlement in the Promised Land was beyond

the powers of men and women whose will had been crushed by bondage. This was a task for the new generation, born free, hardened in youth by the toughness of desert life, who would battle an enemy with courage and skill.

He was wise enough to recognize that what he and the former slaves had done had been vital; and that in spite of all their failings and their grumbling, it had been their extraordinary struggle amidst bitter suffering which had brought their children within reach of the fruits. He and they together had laid the foundations of their freedom, their unique religion and their nationhood. It was now up to the young to undertake the next crucial struggle and gain independence in their own land. He trusted them. He was heartened by their strength of will and their readiness for self-sacrifice. He also had confidence in the man who would lead them: his successor would be Joshua. He had no doubt that, if they remained faithful to the Lord's Covenant, they would prove equal to their task.

FAREWELL

It was with these thoughts in mind that Moses

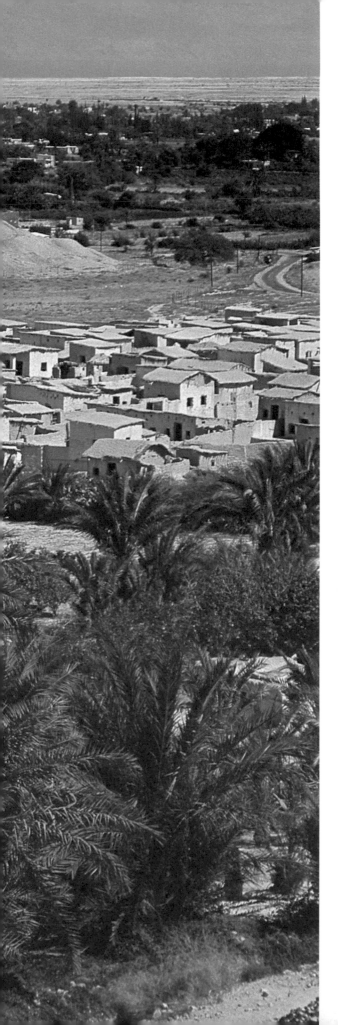

The city and plain of Jericho, looking east. The sand-colored ridge in the upper part of the photograph is the mound which holds the ancient remains.

offered his words of farewell to the people of Israel. (They are recorded in the first person in the chapters of Deuteronomy.) To the children and grandchildren of those who had started the freedom march, he spoke as Moses the great educator. He told them the dramatic story of the Exodus and the journey through the wilderness, and urged them never to forget it. As Moses the Prophet and Law-Giver, he recalled the Commandments and the Covenant Code, and expanded the ordinances. Finally, as the wise and experienced leader, Moses gave them sage advice on their future behavior when they came to settle in their land.

He ended his religious instruction with what have become the most noted words in the Hebrew Prayer Book, uttered to this day, after three thousand three hundred years, by Jews throughout the world: "Hear, O Israel: The Lord our God is one Lord: and you shall love the Lord your God with all your heart, and with all your soul, and with all your might. And these words, which I command you this day, shall be upon your heart; and you shall teach them diligently to your

175

children…" (Deuteronomy 6:4–7). Of immeasurable importance was his instruction to teach "these words… to your children". It was faithfully respected and carried out in all the generations that followed, and is certainly one of the major reasons for the survival of the Jewish people — and for the regained State of Israel in our own day.

Moses then went up "unto the mountain of Nebo, to the top of Pisgah, which is opposite Jericho", and there he was given a view of the future Land of Israel. It was a glorious sun-lit scene. Below him, the river Jordan sparkled as it flowed between rich green banks to the glittering Dead Sea. Beyond it was the fertile plain of Jericho. And rising in the distance were the hills of Jerusalem and the central mountain range. He gazed in wonder at all that he saw, content that he had accomplished his part of the divine mission. But there was a certain sadness in his heart, as he turned to go down from the mountain top, that for him the trek had ended, and it would not be given him to enter what his eyes had been allowed to glimpse — the Promised Land.

There, "in a valley in the land of Moab", Moses died, "but no man knows the place of his burial unto this day" (Deuteronomy 34:6). (It is still not known, though it must be in the vicinity of Mount Nebo, some seven miles beyond the northeastern edge of the Dead Sea.) He was mourned for thirty days, and then the children of Israel, under the leadership of Joshua, readied themselves to cross the Jordan — and fight the first Jewish War of Independence.

176

CHAPTER 12 THE BATTLES

In which the new generation fight their way through the Promised Land with courage, stratagems and original tactics.

Big wars and little wars, world wars and local wars; if it is not one, it is the other. As I write these words, there is still fighting in the Far East. By the time you read them, the chances are that if fighting has stopped there, it will have broken out somewhere else. War seems always to be with us, even in the civilized world of today, where there is a United Nations Organization; where most countries have fixed and recognized boundaries; where most have ordered societies, most cooperate with each other in a variety of fields, and all their political leaders claim, at least, that peace is their ideal, and military aggression a horror to be outlawed.

Small wonder that in the primitive world of the ancient Middle East, war was even more common. There was no United Nations. There were no newspapers, radio or television, no advanced, pro-peace public opinion that could make itself felt. There was no ordered society. There was no safety and no security. The weak were at the mercy of the strong, and the strong tried to get stronger through battle, whether it was the petty king of a city or the mighty ruler of an empire. Anarchy prevailed.

In those days, too, there were huge spaces, comparatively empty, in the Middle East, with no fixed boundaries, a small settled population and wandering tribesmen. People journeyed long distances from one region to another, wiping out others on the way or being themselves wiped out, raiding a village and moving on to raid another, or being themselves defeated and either killed or made slaves by the conqueror. Sometimes, when a raid was successful, they would take over the village and lands they had conquered, and settle down themselves — until they in turn were raided, killed, enslaved or driven off by stronger newcomers.

This was the pattern in Canaan at that time. Its sparse population consisted of nomadic tribes still continuing their wandering lives, and other nomads who had taken over villages and cities and settled down. Thus, the inhabitants of the country were a collection of different groups of varied origins, in frequent conflict with one another. Each tried to guard what it had conquered, and gain strength to grab the possessions of a weaker neighboring group. New arrivals

So Joshua arose, and all the fighting men, to go up to Ai (Joshua 8:3)

Remains of the ancient city of Ai, the second
walled city which Joshua captured by a military stratagem.

were feared if they were strong; if they were weak, they were looked on eagerly as a source of loot, women and slaves. Joshua and his people were determined not to fall into the latter category.

THE INGENIOUS COMMANDER

The military campaign was to be long and tough. The strategy of entering the Promised Land from the east proved wise, for this region was less heavily populated and defended less strongly than the coastal plain in the southwest. But it still offered stubborn obstacles. Not least were the stout defensive walls round the cities. The armies of powerful empires used battering rams to break through such walls. The poorly armed Israelites had no such weapons.

Nevertheless, they enjoyed several advantages which were to be decisive. They were led by Joshua, and Moses had chosen well when he had spotted this young man early on during the wilderness journey and picked him as his aide. Joshua showed himself to be an ingenious military commander. He planned with wisdom and imagination, and operated on the battlefield with skill and daring.

The forces he commanded were united as they had never been before. This was due very much to the efforts of Moses. Another important reason was that the people were now at war — as they would be for many years ahead — and a people is more united in war than it is in peace. But perhaps the principal factor was that all were bound by the Covenant with God, by their distinctive faith. This made them very different from other nomadic tribes, and gave them results — victory, and a future — which other nomads failed to achieve. It fashioned the Israelites into a more compact force than the enemies they faced. It gave them a higher sense of purpose, and this heightened their stamina, their tenacity and their fighting morale. It was their unique faith, as the biblical scholar John Bright says, "which set Israel off from her environment and made her the distinctive and creative phenomenon that she was."

THE WALLS TUMBLE DOWN

The Israelites, still stationed on the east bank

180

vaht audita restructione cunitarum hieti co. 7 hii epls Gabaon prinne maliciose cogirauit ne
ad Josue dissimibus q̄ essent illarum regionum incolla. er quasi uemens de longinquo in euius
signum acceperunt ueltes antiquas er fractos calceos. er panes picuustos. atqz ita uementes ad exerci
tum Josue. p̄ huiusmoch cautelam acceperunt cum eo federis ut socam essent. nec ocederentur ab eo:–

The region between the hills of Judah and the mountains of Ephraim which would be settled later by the tribe of Benjamin.

of the Jordan, were now ready to start their campaign. But one small operation was required before they could cross the river. Joshua had been one of the twelve intelligence agents sent in earlier by Moses to spy out the land, and so he knew something of the terrain over which he would be battling. But he now needed up-to-date information, particularly about the first obstacle he would need to hurdle. This was Jericho, which lay astride the route he would need to take to get to the interior of the country. Joshua wanted to know about the defenses of the city, and also about the spirit and morale of its inhabitants. So he sent in a small unit — two men — to find out.

They managed to get into Jericho quite openly, probably by claiming that they were merchants or travelers, and using an appropriate disguise. (The full report appears in Chapter 2 of the Book of Joshua.) They lodged with a harlot named Rahab, and it was she who hid them when the authorities started searching for them, and she who helped them to escape. They were soon able to return to Joshua and tell him what they

had learned of the city's fighting power.

After Joshua had heard their detailed report, he gave the order to his people to move. They crossed the Jordan at a small ford just north of the Dead Sea. They met no opposition, and continued to Gilgal, situated between the river and Jericho. Here they set up their base. And it was here, in Gilgal, that they celebrated the Passover Festival, their first in the Promised Land. Nothing could have strengthened their spirits more dramatically than this ritual remembrance of the Exodus. So far, the Lord's promises had been fulfilled. They were now here, on the soil of their land. True, they were not settled yet. There was grim fighting ahead. But they could face it with confidence, and with certainty that they would emerge the victors. It was a fit and courageous body of fighters, filled with religious zeal, who set out shortly afterwards for Jericho.

What followed was the well-known story of the collapse of Jericho's walls (told in Chapter 6 of the Book of Joshua). They fell amidst the trumpeting and the shouting on the seventh day, after the Israelite forces had

silently marched round the city on each of the previous six days. Many Bible critics have dismissed this biblical report as a pleasant legend, not to be taken seriously. But this is because most of them know little about war, and have failed to grasp the thinking behind Joshua's battle plan. It seems clear that he worked out the action he would take after listening to the report of his two spies. And he based his plan on what they told him of the strength of Jericho's walls and the state of mind of its people.

The Bible does not tell us all that they said. But it does mention that they found the men of Jericho "panic stricken". It was very understandable. The Jerichoans would have heard of the amazing Israelite victories over the Amorites and Bashanites across the river, and this alone would have shown them that the strangers were a force to be reckoned with. It is reasonable to suppose that this vital information, together with the probable report that the city walls were too thick to penetrate, was enough to give Joshua an idea of what he proposed to do. By the time he reached Gilgal, he would have worked

out that the people of Jericho would by now be even more terrified. For they would have watched the strange and frightening sight of the Israelites crossing the Jordan and moving forward to encamp at Gilgal. (Even today, from the ruins of ancient Jericho one has a clear view of the river across the plain.) They would now be wondering whether the Israelites meant to bypass Jericho or make straight for it.

It was probably at just about this point that the ruler of Jericho would have remembered that some weeks earlier there had been two strangers inside the city walls who had been seen entering the house of Rahab but who had escaped. Just as he would have been putting two and two together and concluding that the two men must have been Hebrew spies, he would suddenly have spotted the Israelite force advancing on his city. Knowing what had happened to King Sihon and King Og, he and his people must have been filled with gloom. But they had no doubt found reassurance in the strength of their ramparts.

Since Joshua possessed none of the means to breach, scale or tunnel under walls, he had to strike at Jericho's weakest point — the morale of its people. This was the one element in which his own force outmatched the men of Jericho, and he therefore thought up an attack plan suited to this circumstance. In modern times we have heard that often in the opening stage of a battle, the enemy is "softened up" by an artillery barrage. Joshua "softened" them by what would be known today as psychological warfare. It was really a method to weaken the enemy's resistance. What he did was to use a stratagem — a military ruse, or trick — to lull them into a false sense of security and then spring a surprise.

This theory is suggested by the noted archaeologist Yigael Yadin, who is also a former general and Chief of Staff of the Israel Army. It will be recalled that in the biblical report, Joshua ordered his army to march round the city walls once daily for six days running. They were accompanied by the Ark of the Covenant led by seven priests carrying seven *shofarim* — trumpets made of rams' horns. They blew their trumpets as they marched, but the troops were told not to

utter a sound. On the seventh day, they made seven circuits of the city. During the seventh, Joshua suddenly ordered the army to shout, and make a dash for the walls. The defenses were overcome, and Jericho fell.

Yadin says that by parading his men silently on the first day, Joshua had confused and worried the Jericho defenders. Doing the same the second day, again without taking any action, had kept them guessing. By the end of the third day, they had begun to relax. By the fourth and fifth, they may well have thought that the Israelites were engaged in a harmless drill. By the seventh day, expecting the "drill" to end as before, the men of Jericho were startled by the fierce shouting that now accompanied the eerie trumpeting of the rams' horns. And they panicked when the Israelites suddenly broke ranks and began rushing the walls. They were too terror-struck to put up a systematic defense, and Jericho was taken.

MILITARY TRICKS

The Jericho victory may have made Joshua over-confident and his men somewhat careless. Their next target, which lay along their route to the interior of the country, was the hill city of Ai. Joshua sent out a reconnaissance patrol, and they reported back that its defenses were rather weak. This proved to be very poor military intelligence, for when a small force was sent up the slopes to attack the city in the conventional way, they were beaten back. This was a humbling experience, but useful. It warned Joshua and his men to be wary and watchful at all times during a war. It also reminded the commander that so long as he was without the equipment to penetrate walled fortifications, he still had to rely on stratagems.

He tried again, this time with a larger force, and with a cunning plan. It was based on Joshua's reasoning of how the enemy would react to his initial moves. His aim, since he could not batter the walls of Ai, was to induce its defenders to leave them and come out. He therefore sent a unit up the hillside under cover of night with orders to take up hidden positions behind the city — between Ai and Bethel. In the morning, Joshua with his main force appeared in front of the city. After a brief skirmish, they turned tail and fled. The soldiers of Ai, contemptuous of the Israelites whom they had sent packing a few days earlier and who seemed now again to be on the run, promptly pursued them, as Joshua foresaw that they would. He and his men continued their flight, drawing the forces of Ai farther away from their city. Suddenly, Joshua flashed a signal, by waving his spear, to his unit lying in hidden ambush. They quickly left the positions they had taken up during the night, rushed into the now undefended Ai and set it alight. When the pursuers looked back and saw the smoke rising from their city, they were dumbfounded. And they were even more shocked when Joshua's forces, who had seemed to be in full retreat, suddenly stopped, turned, and attacked them. (This classic military ruse is recorded in Chapter 8 of the Book of Joshua.)

Not every engagement was won by military wile and not every target was a fortified city. There was also a good deal of hard conventional fighting in open country, and the Israelites became stronger, more skillful and

Sun, stand thou still at Gibeon, and thou Moon in the valley of Aijalon

(Joshua 10:12)

The Valley of Aijalon, roughly midway between Jerusalem and Tel Aviv. This is where Joshua bade the moon stand still, so that he would have more hours of daylight to pursue and catch the five kings who had attacked Gibeon. They were in full retreat, but Joshua feared that, with nightfall, they might escape under cover of darkness and regroup to counter-attack.

more experienced with each battle. They got more and better weapons, captured from the enemy, with each victory, and they also were able to establish advance bases as more territory came under their control. Their military successes had the additional effect of weakening the spirits of potential enemies, and several hastened to make peaceful agreements with Joshua to avoid combat.

One of them was a group of four cities, headed by Gibeon, who secured an alliance with Joshua by trickery. The Gibeonites lived in the hill country a few miles northwest of Jerusalem, and they controlled the route down into the lowlands through the valley of Aijalon. This was the obvious route which Joshua would be taking to reach the coastal plain, and the Gibeonites were afraid that he would first attack their positions on the heights in order to protect his movement down to the coast. They reckoned that they stood no chance against the victor of Jericho and Ai, and so they resorted to a ruse.

They picked a number of their elders and disguised them as travelers who had been on a long journey. The elders put on old and

torn clothes and worn-out sandals, covered their donkeys with old sacks, and carried wine skins that were split and patched and bread that was dry and moldy. They then set out as a delegation for the main Israelite base at Gilgal, and asked to see the commander. "We have come from a far country", they told Joshua; but even there they had heard of his military wonders under the guidance "of the Lord your God", and they wanted his friendship. "So now make a covenant with us" (Joshua 9:6), they begged him.

Some of Joshua's people doubted their story, and wondered aloud whether the visitors perhaps were not what they seemed to be, but were in fact local people. The delegation, however, pointed to their tattered clothing and moldy food, which had been new and fresh when they had set out but had rotted during their long journey from their distant land. They put on a very convincing act, and Joshua was taken in. He granted them a treaty of friendship, and the covenant was sealed with solemn oaths.

Three days later the Israelites discovered that they had been tricked, and Joshua with his units marched on Gibeon. The Gibeonites expected to be killed for their deceit, but they told Joshua that they had done what they did out of fear, and they asked forgiveness. "We are your servants", they told him; "and now, behold, we are in your hand: do as it seems good and right in your sight to do to us" (Joshua 9:8, 25). His people were angry, but Joshua insisted that an oath was an oath, and the Gibeonites were not harmed. However, as a punishment for their guile, Joshua told them they would be "hewers of wood and drawers of water for the congregation and for the altar of the Lord."

THE SUN STANDS STILL

The Gibeonites' treaty with Joshua greatly disturbed several nearby Canaanite rulers who had asked them to join in united battle against the Israelites. Five of these petty kings, ruling the cities of Jerusalem, Hebron, Jarmuth, Lachish and Eglon, now felt themselves exposed to an Israelite assault as a result of the Gibeonite desertion. They were too weak to attack the Israelites, but they could take action against Gibeon, "for it had made peace with Joshua and with the people of Israel." This league of five cities thereupon moved north through the hills and set siege to Gibeon and the three other cities in its group. The Gibeonites immediately sent urgent appeals for help to Joshua, quoting their treaty of mutual friendship. Joshua responded swiftly.

He led his men on a night march and took the attackers by surprise, assaulting them simultaneously at different points. They were thrown into confusion, and rushed in headlong retreat down the mountains through the descent of Beth Horon into the vale of Aijalon. The Israelites went after them in hot pursuit. But darkness was now approaching, and Joshua was worried that they might either get away, or re-group under cover of night and stage a counter-attack. He needed a few more hours of light, and it was then that he made his celebrated appeal to the Lord: "Sun, stand thou still at Gibeon, and thou Moon in the valley of Aijalon" (Joshua 10:12). The five kings were killed and their armies vanquished.

The way to the south was now open, though Joshua prudently bypassed the strong fortresses of Gezer and Jerusalem (despite the death of its king), and advanced into the southern coastal plain. He then followed the strategy of first seizing the forts which protected the approaches to the southern hill country, and this enabled him to go on to conquer Makkedah, Libnah, Lachish and Eglon one after the other. He now had a clear route through the passes, and he wheeled east to assault and capture the important city of Hebron. He ended this stage of his southern campaign by turning back to the southwest and taking Debir.

Joshua now moved his army north, towards Galilee. The most powerful ruler in this region was the king of Hazor. At the approach of the Israelites, he gathered together the neighboring rulers and their armies, and they decided on joint action. Instead of waiting for Joshua to come up to their cities and pick them off singly, they would all go forth as a united army and defeat him in open battle. So they hoped. The rival forces clashed in heavy combat "at the waters of Merom"

And Joshua turned back... and took Hazor... for Hazor formerly was the head of all those kingdoms *(Joshua 11:10)*

Stone monuments, and a relief of a lion on a block of basalt (left), which were discovered in the remains of a 14th–13th century BC Canaanite temple during an archaeological dig at Hazor. Also unearthed were these ruins of a public building (right). Hazor was the largest Canaanite city conquered by Joshua.

(Joshua 11:5), and the Israelites won. They were, after all, the most battle-hardened veterans in the country by now. Joshua then went on to Hazor itself. It overlooked the Huleh Valley and controlled an important stretch of "the way of the sea", the main road from Egypt to Damascus. Though well-fortified, it failed to stand up to the onslaught of the Israelites and was destroyed. (Evidence of this destruction was found a few years ago in a remarkable archaeological dig carried out by Yigael Yadin.)

Joshua had led his forces with brilliant generalship through successful campaigns in the center, the south and the north of the country. By the time he died, the Israelite tribes were firmly established in the land. It is clear, however, from certain passages in the Book of Joshua and from the whole of Judges, that the conquest was not completed in Joshua's time. The extreme north of Canaan — the region now known as Syria and Lebanon — as well as the coastal plain remained unconquered. Several strongholds in the center, like Jerusalem and Gezer, remained enemy pockets within Israel. But

as a result of Joshua's actions, the tribes would eventually gain mastery over the entire country and develop their distinctive national and religious life.

Throughout the fighting, Joshua the military commander never forgot that he was also a successor to Moses the Law-giver, and he was equally concerned with the religious and ethical development of his people. Shortly after the battle for Ai, he gathered them in solemn assembly on the slopes of Mounts Ebal and Gerizim, above Shechem (present-day Nablus). And "he wrote there upon the stones a copy of the law of Moses... And afterward he read all the words of the law, the blessings and cursings, according to all that is written in the book of the law. There was not a word of all that Moses commanded, which Joshua read not before all the congregation of Israel..." (Joshua 8:32–35).

Joshua held repeated gatherings of this kind, constantly reminding them of their Covenant with the Lord and urging them to respect the commandments. As they extended their territorial control, they naturally found themselves with more neighbors. All were pagan, and Joshua was worried that his people might adopt the customs and religious practices of these other peoples. He therefore cautioned the Israelites never to "make mention of the name of their gods, nor cause to swear by them, neither serve them, nor bow yourselves unto them: But cleave unto the Lord your God" and remain loyal to the faith of Israel.

CHAPTER 13 TILLERS OF THE SOIL

In which soldiers become successful settlers,
but almost lose the fruits of their victory.

Now that the military campaigns were over, the tribes had to turn themselves from fighters to farmers and start settling the country (though without losing the art of self-defense). Each tribe was given a special region. Reuben, Gad and part of the tribe of Manasseh had been allowed by Moses to live in the lands on the east bank of the Jordan which had been conquered before they had crossed the river into Canaan. However, he had laid down the condition that their fighting men would join the other tribes in the coming battles for the country, and only at the end of the war would they return to their families. They could now do so. The tribe of Judah was given the land south of Jerusalem. Ephraim and the other part of Manasseh, the tribes of the sons of Joseph, were allotted the areas south and north of Shechem in the center of the country. The rest of the land was divided by lot among the remaining seven tribes. The lots were drawn at a special assembly held at Shiloh.

It was to Shiloh that Joshua had brought the Ark of the Covenant, there that he had "set up the tabernacle of the congregation" (Joshua 18:1). Shiloh was probably the first

site of Jewish pilgrimage, where "the whole congregation of the children of Israel" would gather to fulfill the original command (in Exodus 23:17 and 34:23 and in Deuteronomy 16:16): "Three times a year all your males shall appear before the Lord your God at the place he will choose: at the feast of unleavened bread, at the feast of weeks, and at the feast of booths." [During almost the next two centuries, the Ark would be moved from one tribal center to another, so that it remained for a period with each tribe. The center of worship for all the tribes would then be wherever the Ark was established, and this would also be the main meeting place for the tribal representatives. The Bible records that the last temporary site of the Ark was again Shiloh, towards the end of the 11th century BC, and this suggests the likelihood that Shiloh was the chief religious center for most of this period. At the beginning of the 10th century, King David brought the Ark to Jerusalem, and from then on Jerusalem became its permanent home and the permanent center of Jewish pilgrimage.]

The biblical record shows that the Israelites

Moses charged the people the same day, saying... these shall stand upon Mount Gerizim to bless the people... And these shall stand upon Mount Ebal for the curse

(Deuteronomy 27:12, 13)

Mount Ebal (left) and Mount Gerizim (below),
the two mountains above Shechem where Joshua
held a religious ceremony and read to
the people the Laws handed down at Sinai.
In accordance with the command of Moses
(in Deuteronomy 27:12, 13), he proclaimed the blessings,
associated with Gerizim, and the curses, associated
with Ebal. To this day, Mount Ebal
is barren, while Mount Gerizim is green and fruitful.

the people of Israel assembled at Shiloh, and set up the tent of the meeting there; the land lay subdued before them (Joshua 18:1)

Ancient Hebrew writing on a piece of pottery (left) found at archaeological excavations a few miles south of Tel Aviv. Remains of a site of worship in Shiloh (right). It was at Shiloh that Joshua set up the Ark of the Covenant and established there the first religious center for the tribes of Israel in the Promised Land.

quickly adapted themselves to their new life of farming, and they started developing the land with the same energy with which they had fought for it. This is confirmed by the archaeological evidence. As the great American biblical scholar W. F. Albright pointed out: "Archaeological excavation and exploration are throwing increasing light on the character of the earliest Israelite occupation, about 1200 BC. First it is important to note that the new inhabitants settled in towns like Bethel... only a short time after their destruction. The Israelites were thus far from being characteristic nomads or even semi-nomads, but had reached a stage where they were ready to settle down, tilling the soil and dwelling in stone houses. A second main point is that the new Israelite occupation was incomparably more intensive than was the preceding Canaanite one. All over the hill country we find remains of Iron-Age (12th century BC) villages which had not been inhabited in the Late Bronze Age (15th–13th centuries BC) and many of which had never been occupied previously." In these places, the Israelites were the first settlers.

After these things Joshua the son of Nun, the servant of the Lord, died... And they buried him in his own inheritance at Timnath-serah, which is in the hill country of Ephraim (Joshua 24:29, 30)

The death of Joshua. From a 13th century illustrated manuscript in the Pierpoint Morgan collection.

A STRANGE IRONY

Joshua, like Moses before him, had commanded supreme authority over all the tribes, and he had held this central position of leadership until his death. When he died, the position was not filled. The community was without an overall leader. It was a strangely ironical situation in this initial period of Israelite settlement: after all their sufferings and achievements, the people had returned almost to the same tribal framework in which they had lived in Egypt and during their early years in the wilderness. Each tribe was again virtually independent. They had no political capital, no central government or administration, no central army. Each tribe was now settled in its own tribal area, concerned with developing and adapting itself to the new conditions of life in its own region. None had an urgent pressing concern for the welfare of the other tribes. Tribal society was once again largely patriarchal, with the affairs of the tribe conducted by the clan and tribal leaders in accordance with tribal tradition. Thus, while Moses had tried to unify them and Joshua had succeeded in

doing so during the war years, it would seem that they had now broken up again into their former twelve fragments, each a world unto itself.

But there was a crucial difference: because of the dramatic ceremony at Sinai, they were now a confederation of tribes bound together and united in their collective Covenant with God. Furthermore, added to their common faith was the common memory of the fantastic wonders, divinely inspired, of their immediate past. Thus, however much political independence each tribe enjoyed, all looked up to the central shrine, the Ark of the Covenant; and Shiloh — or wherever else the Ark happened to be — became the focal point of the confederacy. Here the tribal elders would meet one another at least at festival times; and they would no doubt use the occasion to discuss problems common to all the tribes, possibly clear up inter-tribal disputes, and perhaps agree to a limited cooperation on matters of mutual interest.

In the early years, however, such contacts were informal, and rarely led to a common policy or action of major importance. It is

200

اینجا جون جانِ اسیرد و از غم درگذشت

ؤ aliter Iosue composito statu filiorum
Israhel moritur.

אז רואים רחוק כרדן יהושע

Jewish pilgrimage to the Western Wall of the Temple Mount again became possible with the re-unification of Jerusalem during the 1967 Six Day War. Ever since King David brought the Ark of the Law to Jerusalem, it was there that "the congregation of Israel" yearned to celebrate their three Pilgrim Festivals: Passover, Pentecost and Succoth.

Deborah, a prophetess... was judging Israel at that time. She used to sit under the palm of Deborah between Ramah and Bethel (Judges 4:4, 5)

It was under a palm tree in the region of Ephraim that Deborah the Judge would sit and give guidance to the people of Israel. She devoted herself to promoting unity among the tribes, and at a time of acute danger, she spurred them to military victory.

easy to understand why. At that time, soon after the conquest, there was no serious military danger. Any one of the tribes, with its experienced fighters, could cope on its own with the occasional raid by marauding nomads. None of the attacks was heavy enough to require the help of another tribe. (It is probable that each tribe soon maintained its own militia, made up of warriors drawn from each family and clan on a quota system.) It is also reasonable to assume that the tribal elders must have been pleased to command the kind of authority such leaders had not enjoyed since the pre-Moses days. They welcomed autonomy, and favored the idea that each tribe should plow its own furrow. Indeed, some were so anxious to further the interests of their own tribe that they came into conflict with other tribes, over such matters as boundary disputes. The Bible provides a record of several grim and quite bloody clashes between them.

A NEW DANGER

Within a few years, however, inter-tribal cooperation was to reappear, even though it

Go, gather your men at Mount Tabor ... And I will draw out Sisera, the general of Jabin's army ... and I will give him into your hand   *(Judges 4:6, 7)*

Mount Tabor (left), the hill in the Valley of Jezreel. This is where the general Barak, at the urging of Deborah, assembled his Israelite forces and gave battle to the army of Sisera, the commanding general of "Jabin king of Canaan". The archaeological site of biblical Megiddo (below), strategically situated at the western end of the valley, was close to the battlefield where the decisive clash took place.

205

The Valley of Jezreel, as seen from the top of Mount Tabor, looking south.

was only periodic. It was brought about by the invasion of new and vigorous enemies, and also by old enemies who had recovered their strength. These threatened the very existence of all the tribes, and this menace was to have the eventual effect of hammering them into national unity.

In the second half of the 12th century BC came the Philistines from the region of the Aegean Sea. They were a hardy and energetic people, who landed on the coast, settled in the coastal plain, and tried, after a time, to press inland and seize Israelite territory. Then came the Midianites from the far south, who had learned how to bring camels under human control and used them to carry out long-range raids with devastating results. There was also trouble from those Canaanite city-states which had not been conquered; from the Arameans who came in from the Syrian desert; and from the kings of Moab and Ammon on the other side of the river Jordan. Some of these peoples thought they stood a good chance of overthrowing the Israelites by gobbling them up tribe by tribe.

Fortunately for the Israelites, they usually

206

The kings... fought... by the waters of Megiddo

(Judges 5:19)

The 9th century BC water tunnel of Megiddo (with a boarded floor and electric lighting recently added for visitors). The fresh water spring was outside the city walls, so the inhabitants bored this 300-feet tunnel from the center of the city, which enabled them to reach their source of water in time of siege without being spotted by the enemy. They also camouflaged the outside approaches to the spring so that the besieging forces would not notice it.

— though not always — managed to see the danger in time. In such moments of acute crisis, all, or several, of the tribes would forget their differences and join together to do battle for the common cause. They would rally behind one of their people whose special qualities had given him or her a reputation which had impressed even members of other tribes; and this person would lead them in the struggle against the enemy.

These leaders were known as Judges, and they would call upon the tribes to carry out their duties under the Covenant, and rouse them to fight for the survival of the whole community and for their faith. These Judges commanded no formal authority. They could do nothing if any tribe refused to obey them (as some did). Their only power was the power of their personality, their words and their example. Their only punishment was a curse — or contempt. Nor was their leadership permanent. It lasted only for as long as there was danger (though in some cases it was extended). But while it lasted, the confederacy of tribes took on the pattern of a united nation.

As soon as they felt the danger had passed, the people would slide back to their former state of independent tribes, and the leader no longer enjoyed overall authority. After a time, the idea of unity was forgotten, each tribe went its own way, the people became less respectful of the Commandments and of their religious duties, and some even found the practices of their pagan neighbors more tempting than the call of the Covenant. It was about such periods that the Bible laments: "there was no king [leader] in Israel; every man did what was right in his own eyes." This moral slackness was often accompanied by a dangerous illusion of safety, and a lowered alertness to the aims and plans of their enemies. It usually ended with a renewed threat of attack, a further period of danger — and the spontaneous choice of another Judge.

The Judges were not drawn from any special tribe, nor from any particular class or profession. Some had not even been leaders of their own tribes. Not all were men: one of the most outstanding was Deborah. Some had become widely known for acts of bravery, some for their wisdom, some for their

A general view of Zorah and Eshtaol, to the west
of Jerusalem. This is the region where Samson was born,
spent his childhood, and developed that strength and bravery which
were later to mark his legendary deeds against the Philistines.

*the woman bore a son, and called his name Samson...
the boy grew... the Spirit of the Lord began to stir
him in Mahaneh-dan, between Zorah and Eshtaol*

(Judges 13:24, 25)

The recently discovered water system of ancient
Gibeon (El Jib), six miles northwest of Jerusalem.
Archaeology has shown that the Israelites were
responsible for the first intensive development of the
land, particularly of the hill country. Water was the
key to this farming progress, and they found
advanced ways of saving and storing water.

holiness. But hero or sage, man or woman, all
possessed a rare natural quality: they gener-
ated a public feeling that they were touched
by the hand of God. They had what is known
as charisma, a divine grace, special gifts of
mind and character which produced a sense
of trust. The respect and prestige they commanded cut across tribal boundaries.

When crisis came, there would be a general
demand that they take over the leadership of
the people.

CHAPTER 14 THE REMARKABLE TWELVE

In which a heroic succession of men — and one woman — saves the nation in moments of peril.

The biblical Book of Judges records the names of twelve who periodically "judged Israel" in those days. Six of them receive little more than a mention, so that we cannot know the conditions of their times, what enemies they faced or for what special deeds they became famous. The six about whom the Bible has more to say, and were evidently the most important, were Othniel, Ehud, Deborah, Gideon, Jephthah and Samson. Of these, Deborah and Gideon were clearly the most outstanding, and Samson was the most colorful.

In the biblical record, Othniel is listed as the first of the warrior-Judges to have been "raised up" by the Lord as "a deliverer for the people of Israel" (Judges 3:9). But we are told little beyond the fact that when the Israelites were being attacked by a certain King Cushan-rishataim, Othniel led the tribes to war against him and was victorious. He is believed to have been active at the beginning of the 12th century BC.

THE LEFT-HANDED SWORDSMAN

He was followed by Ehud, a member of the tribe of Benjamin, whose region of settlement lay between Judah, to the south, and Ephraim, to the north. In his day, the tribes in his part of the country were being hard pressed by the Moabites, who had conquered territory on the east bank of the Jordan and were driving westwards, across the river. With the help of neighboring kingdoms, they had penetrated to "the city of palms" (Judges 3:13). This was Jericho, and that was where the king of Moab installed himself and put the local Israelites under his control. They were forced to pay tribute to him — a sum of money or its equivalent, acknowledging his mastery. It was in Jericho that Ehud carried out a daring exploit, paving the way for a successful military action which restored Israelite freedom. He arrived at the king's headquarters bringing tribute. When that ceremony was over, he secured a private audience with the king, smuggled a dagger into the throne chamber, and slew the enemy ruler.

Yigael Yadin has a fascinating explanation, based on scholarly detective work, of how Ehud got past the king's guards without being disarmed. If you read the biblical account

The head of a Philistine coffin, shaped like a man, dating back to the 12th century BC. It was discovered at archaeological excavations in Beth Shan, near the Jordan Valley.

(Judges 3:12–30), you will see that it contains the details that Ehud was "left-handed", and made himself a sword with "two edges, of a cubit length" (fifteen inches) which he fastened "under his raiment upon his right thigh". Most scholars tended to dismiss these facts as only of mild interest; they simply added a little color to the story of Ehud. Yadin, however, realized that these were key clues. At that period, he says, the standard sword in the region was the long curved type. Such a weapon could not have been hidden from the guards, and so Ehud, for the act he had in mind, made one that could. Describing it as two edged showed that it was a straight sword; and the record of its length showed that it was only a little longer than a dagger, and easy to hide. Underlining the detail that it was fastened to his right side — because Ehud was left-handed — meant that in searching for weapons, the guards would have missed it, for the left was the side on which the ordinary — right-handed — person wore his sword.

After killing the king, Ehud locked the doors from the inside and escaped through

*the angel of the Lord came and sat under the oak...
which belonged to Joash... as his son Gideon was
beating out wheat in the wine press, to hide it from
the Midianites* (Judges 6:11)

Gideon was separating the grain from the husks when he received the divine call which thrust him into battle command and the eventual leadership of his people. In some Arab villages in today's Israel, the ancient method of winnowing wheat is still followed.

the porch. He hurried to the hill country of Ephraim, sounded the alert which assembled the tribesmen, and led the men down to the river Jordan, where they seized the fords. The Moabite troops in and around Jericho on the west bank were thus cut off from their own land. Faced by this unexpected situation, and already stunned by the death of their king and commander, they were thrown into confusion, and were quickly routed by the Israelites.

THE WARRIOR-DIPLOMAT

Jephthah is popularly thought of as a rough and ready soldier, and he is usually remembered only for his terrible vow (Judges 11:31) which led to the sacrifice of his daughter. He was, indeed, a tough military leader, but he resorted to action only when diplomacy failed. In his day, the enemy were the Ammonites, who had become the new masters in trans-Jordan. Like their predecessors, they, too, hoped to take advantage of the tribal separatism among the Israelites to seize their land. They started by harassing, then attacking and finally overrunning the region settled

by the Israelites in Gilead, their closest Hebrew neighbors. (Gilead was also in trans-Jordan, to the northwest of Ammon.)

It was then that the elders of Gilead sent for one of their sons, Jephthah, who had been driven from his home by his half-brothers because his mother had been a harlot. Jephthah was now living in the land of Tob, near Gilead, at the head of a band of Gileadites who had followed him. He returned with his own men, and was asked to lead them and the tribal militiamen into battle against Ammon. He agreed. But before going to war, he started negotiations with the Ammonites to try to get them to withdraw peacefully. (The absorbing exchange between the two sides is told in Judges 11:12–28.) Only when the Ammonites refused did Jephthah strike, defeating their army and chasing them across the border into their own territory.

THE ONE-MAN COMMANDO

Samson was quite different. He did not command an army in battle. He acted rather as a one-man commando unit. He is perhaps the least "Judge-like" of all; for although he "judged Israel... twenty years", the account of his actions (Judges 13–16) is less a record of national leadership than of exciting deeds of legendary strength and bravery, and these had a heartening effect on the dwindling morale of his people.

He lived in the early part of the 11th century BC, when the Israelites were being sorely harried by the Philistines. These people had gained rapidly in strength since establishing themselves in the coastal plain in the previous century, and were conducting frequent border raids, which would eventually develop into all-out war. But for the moment these were not on a scale to arouse in the tribes a sense of acute danger and move them to united action. Samson therefore decided to take matters into his own hands, and the Bible gives a vivid account of his exploits.

He slew thirty Philistines in Ashkelon and took their spoil to pay for a bet he lost through Philistine deceit (Judges 14:19). He set fire to Philistine cornfields, vineyards and olive groves by tying firebrands to the tails of three hundred "foxes" (probably jackals) and setting them loose (Judges 15:5). He killed a

216

thousand of the enemy with the "jawbone of an ass" (Judges 15:15). He was finally caught, by treachery, and his eyes were gouged out. Bound in chains, he was brought into the pagan temple in Gaza to be jeered at by the populace in a victory celebration. The "strong man" of Israel had been crushed. But even at the moment of death, the blinded Samson behaved in characteristic fashion. Grasping the pillars that held up the temple, he shouted "let me die with the Philistines" as he tore down the building with his bare hands. The multitude within were killed, and "the dead whom he slew at his death were more than those whom he had slain during his life" (Judges 16:30).

His spectacular deeds touched the hearts and imagination of his people, and contributed in no small measure to their ultimate recognition that their very survival was threatened unless they achieved national unity.

THE LADY UNDER THE PALM TREE

Deborah had none of the glamour of Samson; and she knew nothing of the art of warfare; but her role was more decisive. She it was who inspired her people to take action at a moment of serious danger, and they broke the back of the enemy. However, even she, while securing a ready response from several tribes, did not gain the support of all. While there were some who lived far from the zone of immediate danger, yet who rallied to Deborah's call and rushed to the help of their threatened brothers, there were others who simply stayed home.

The peril in her day came not from a new enemy but from an old foe. She lived in the second half of the 12th century BC, about seventy-five years before Samson. At that time, as the biblical story of Deborah shows (in Judges 4–5), some of the Canaanites who had fought the Israelites in Joshua's time had built up their strength, and had allied themselves under the banner of Sisera, the commanding general of "Jabin king of Canaan". Armed with chariots, which the Israelites did not possess, they tried to conquer the valley of Jezreel, which lies between the center of the country and Galilee in the north. They had already captured some of the

Jerubba'al (that is, Gideon) and all the people who were with him rose early and encamped beside the spring of Harod (Judges 7:1)

The Spring of Harod in the Valley of Jezreel. This is where Gideon carried out his "water test" and picked 300 men from among the thousands who had volunteered to drive off the Midianite raiders. With this small force, and a novel military plan, he led a dramatic and successful commando attack at night against the enemy encamped across the valley. The Spring of Harod is now a National Park.

Israelite settlements at the edge of the valley. If they achieved their aim, they would cut off the central tribal areas from the northern ones. This was clearly the time for the tribes to join together to stop them.

The Bible calls Deborah "a prophetess" who "used to sit under the palm of Deborah between Ramah and Bethel in the hill country of Ephraim; and the people of Israel came up to her for judgement." She was much respected in her own tribe, and had evidently gained wide renown as a wise, farsighted and very determined person. But she had no military knowledge or experience, and this was a situation which called for an army commander. The most noted soldier at the time was Barak. He belonged to the tribe of Naphtali, who were settled in Upper Galilee, and Deborah sent for him. She urged him to mobilize the men of his tribe and of the neighboring tribe of Zebulun and lead them into battle against Sisera. Barak agreed — on one condition: "If you will go with me, I will go; but if you will not go with me, I will not go" (Judges 4:8).

This reply has been taken as a sign of weakness on the part of Barak, and he is not given too prominent a place in the report of the important battle that followed. Indeed, the Bible indicates that because of it, the triumph of slaying Sisera would fall not to him but to a woman. This seems somewhat hard on Barak, who was simply acting within the limits of his capability, limits which he himself recognized. He was a soldier, not a popular leader. He was a skilled and brave combat commander, and he knew how to handle men on the battlefield. But to get them there was the job of the civilian leader. To rouse the tribes to volunteer and go to war required the kind of moral influence and magnetic personality which he did not have. Deborah did. And so he told her that if she would join him in trying to persuade the other tribes, and would accompany him in action, he would take the military command.

The two of them thereupon appealed to the tribes, and those who responded encamped on the slopes of Mount Tabor against the enemy. The hilly ground gave them some protection against the Canaanite chariot squadrons. One cannot tell whether Barak and Deborah timed the meeting between the two forces for the rainy season. But it is clear from the biblical account that there were heavy downpours and this led to the overflowing of a nearby river. The ground of the valley was turned to mud, and this robbed Sisera's forces of their chief advantage — fast movement. The chariots got bogged, and the horse-drawn warriors were stuck. They fell an easy prey to the Israelite foot soldiers who came charging down the hill. The enemy was routed and the threat was lifted from Israel. The commander himself, Sisera, got off his chariot, fled on foot from the battlefield, and sought refuge at a nearby village in the tent of a certain woman named Jael. There he found his death. Jael killed him with a tent peg.

In the victory song of Deborah (Judges 5), there is high praise for those tribes who rallied to the colors. She has particularly warm words to say about Benjamin, whose tribal area was in the south, and the part of Manasseh who lived across the Jordan, for coming from such distances to take part in the fighting. She also pays compliments to Zebulun, "a people that jeoparded their lives to the death"; and to "Naphtali too...". But there is withering scorn for those who stayed away. Among the clans of Reuben "there were great searchings of heart. Why did you tarry among the sheepfolds...?" And the tribe of Dan, "why did he abide with his ships? Asher sat still...!" It was evidently Deborah's aim to encourage the valiant, but above all to shame the selfish into action if and when the House of Israel was again in danger.

A TRUMPET, A TORCH AND A SWORD

Gideon, unlike Barak, was both an inventive military commander and a popular leader. So popular was he, indeed, that the people wished to make him king, calling upon him to "rule over us". But he rejected the offer, saying "the Lord will rule over you" (Judges 8:23). However, the very suggestion that one man be given supreme authority over all the tribes shows that by now they were beginning to recognize the need for a central administration. This was the 11th century BC, about one hundred years after they had started their settlement of the country, and they were prospering.

They were no longer novices at farming. They had learnt the techniques of building. And they had put to good use a very interesting discovery. This was a special lime plaster with which water cisterns could be lined to prevent seepage. Successful water storage was — and is to this day — of key importance in a hot dry land, and it revolutionized agriculture. For the first time, the Israelites were able to cultivate and settle large tracts of their land which before had been bare of crops — and of people. Their prosperity soon invited threats from jealous neighbors and distant marauders, and this no doubt led them to thoughts of closer inter-tribal cooperation under a national leader. They were to get such a leader a few decades later.

The particular problem that troubled them at the time of Gideon were the annual raids at harvest time by the camel-riding Midianites. They would come up from the southern desert, cross the Jordan and steal the Israelite grain just after the granaries had been filled.

This had been going on for several years, and the attackers gained fresh encouragement and confidence with each successful raid. Each year brought them more handsome rewards, and at this rate the Israelite economy would soon be ruined. Gideon, of the tribe of Manasseh, decided to take action when, at the next harvest, a large horde of Midianites crossed to Jordan and brazenly set up camp in the valley of Jezreel.

Gideon rallied the men of his own tribe and of other clans and brought them stealthily to the spring of Harod just opposite the tents of the enemy. Thousands followed him; but for moral and tactical reasons, he needed only relatively few men in the operation he planned. What followed was the "water test", described in Judges 7:4–8. He told them all to drink from the pool, and watched how they did so. Almost all got down on their knees and drew water to their lips in their cupped hands. Three hundred, however, like good old soldiers who do not mind roughing it, care little for the niceties of politeness, and who instinctively expose as little of their bodies as possible to an enemy, flung themselves on the ground face down at the edge of the pool and lapped the water with their tongues, "like a dog". These three hundred were the men Gideon picked. All the rest he sent home.

He then undertook a personal mission at night, accompanied only by his aide Purah, to gather intelligence on the enemy. They crept close enough to the Midianites to hear the guards talking, and took note of the layout of their camp and the change-of-guard times. With the information thus obtained, Gideon worked out a stratagem, which he outlined to his men on his return, and soon put into operation. He equipped each of his three hundred troops with a sword, a trumpet, and a torch hidden inside a jar. (The torch was probably twisted flax or some other material soaked in oil or pitch.) He split his force into three companies, each of one hundred men, gave them detailed orders, and in the middle of the night they made their way quietly to the edge of the sleeping encampment. They were undetected. (The jars hid the flames of the torches.)

The three companies now moved into position on three sides of the Midianite compound. The fourth side, facing east, was left free. Gideon waited until the guards of "the middle watch" were changed. Then, before the new sentries had the chance to rub the sleep from their eyes and get accustomed to the dark, Gideon sounded the signal. He blew a blast on his trumpet, and his men did the same. Blowing their trumpets, they rushed forward, broke the jars containing the lighted torches against the enemy tents, and shouted: "A sword for the Lord and for Gideon." The encampment was soon ablaze. The panic-stricken Midianites, utterly confused by the frightful din of the trumpeting and the shouting, and made frantic by the fire, ran helter-skelter. Those who rushed through the rim of flame in a mad race for safety were met by the swords of Gideon's men. Most of them, however, ran through the unguarded east side — and went on running, towards the river Jordan, as Gideon had planned. He now sent urgent messages to the other tribes to dash to the Jordan to trap them, and he himself set off in pursuit. The victory was complete.

It was so dramatic that Gideon, whose qualities had been known only to the clans of his tribe, was now acclaimed a national hero. The people were particularly impressed by his insistence on using only three hundred men for his initial assault. This showed, as it was intended to show, that he had been guided by the Lord, and it was then that the tribes asked him to be their overall leader. "And the land had rest forty years in the days of Gideon."

The period of the Judges, covering the years of settling in after the Joshua conquest, lasted from the beginning of the 12th century to the latter part of the 11th century BC. It was an agonizing period of transition during which the fate of the Israelites and of their religion hung frequently in the balance. There were times when it was touch-and-go whether the tribes would survive or go under; whether they would hold fast to their unique identity or merge with the surrounding peoples; whether they would remain faithful to their Covenant and Commandments or go after the pagan gods of their neighbors;

and whether or not the national goal would prove stronger than narrow tribal ambitions.

Only with the arrival of the Prophet Samuel, who pulled the tribes together and gave them central direction and leadership, do we find Israel launched on its voyage of creative development. Under Samuel's successors, the kings Saul, David and Solomon, Israel rose to its greatest glory. And then came the Prophets, the visionaries and poets of the five turbulent centuries that followed. It was they who consolidated the unique historic work which Moses had started, and helped give permanent form to the Jewish religion and to Jewish nationhood.

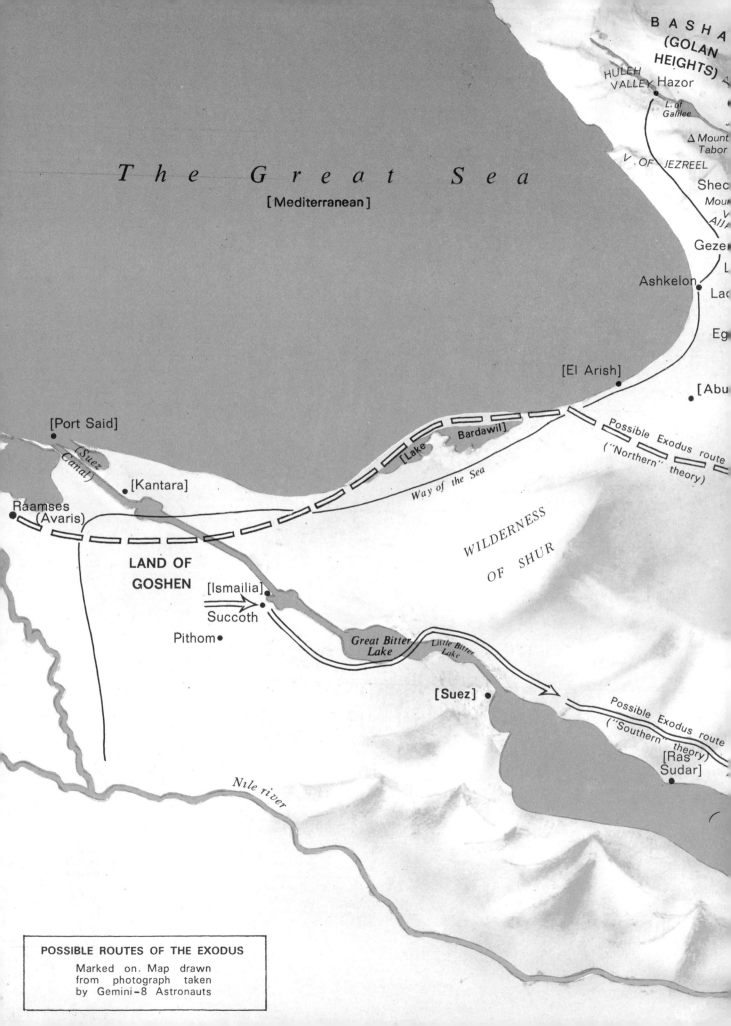

The Great Sea
[Mediterranean]

BASHA
(GOLAN
HEIGHTS)

HULEH
VALLEY Hazor
L. of
Galilee

△ Mount
Tabor

V. OF JEZREEL

Shec
Mou
V.
AIJA

Geze
L.
Ashkelon
Lac

Eg

[El Arish]
[Abu

[Port Said]
(Suez Canal)

[Kantara]

Raamses
(Avaris)

[Lake Bardawil]

Way of the Sea

Possible Exodus route
("Northern" theory)

WILDERNESS
OF SHUR

LAND OF
GOSHEN

[Ismailia]
Succoth

Pithom

Great Bitter
Lake
Little Bitter
Lake

[Suez]

Possible Exodus route
("Southern" theory)
[Ras
Sudar]

Nile river

POSSIBLE ROUTES OF THE EXODUS

Marked on. Map drawn
from photograph taken
by Gemini-8 Astronauts